The Field
Guide to
Extraterrestrials

The Field
Guide to
Extraterrestrials

PATRICK HUYGHE

Illustrated by Harry Trumbore

AVON BOOKS  NEW YORK

**VISIT OUR WEBSITE AT
http://AvonBooks.com**

THE FIELD GUIDE TO EXTRATERRESTRIALS is an original publication of Avon Books. This work has never before appeared in book form.

*001.942
H*

AVON BOOKS
A division of
The Hearst Corporation
1350 Avenue of the Americas
New York, New York 10019

Copyright © 1996 by Patrick Huyghe
Illustrations by Harry Trumbore
Cover illustration by Michael Evans
Published by arrangement with the author
Library of Congress Catalog Card Number: 96-13683
ISBN: 0-380-78128-X

Library of Congress Cataloging in Publication Data:
  A field guide to extraterrestrials : based on actual eyewitness accounts and sightings / Patrick Huyghe : illustrated by Harry Trumbore.
      p. cm.
1. Human-alien encounters.   I. Title.
BF2050.H88   1996   96-13683
001.9'42—dc20   CIP

First Avon Books Trade Printing: October 1996

AVON TRADEMARK REG. U.S. PAT. OFF. AND IN OTHER COUNTRIES, MARCA REGISTRADA, HECHO EN U.S.A.

Printed in the U.S.A.

OPM   10 9 8 7 6 5 4 3 2 1

For Larry W. Bryant

CONTENTS

INTRODUCTION

What Is Real?

Nature lovers have their *National Audubon Society Field Guides.* Science-fiction buffs have *Barlowe's Guide to Extraterrestrials: Great Aliens from Science Fiction Literature.* And folklorists have *A Field Guide to the Little People* by Nancy Arrowsmith and George Moorse. But what about the 5 million Americans who, as a recent Roper Survey suggests, may have been abducted by UFO aliens: What do they have? Well, nothing—until now.

Welcome to *The Field Guide to Extraterrestrials.* Though it may sound like science fiction, it most definitely is not. This volume is based entirely on eyewitness reports of alleged UFO aliens. These reports come from all around the globe and from people of all walks of life—police officers, farmers, doctors, truck drivers, lawyers, pilots, children, and housewives, among others. And these encounters have been going on for a long, long time— at least a century or more.

If these creatures really are what they appear to be— extraterrestrials—then this guide should prove absolutely indispensable, especially if you think you've encountered an extraterrestrial or consider yourself a true-blue UFO believer. It might even be wise to adapt the travel advice of Leonard Maltin and American Express for this field guide: Don't get lost in space without it.

If you're a skeptic, no doubt you'll laugh at this idea. But I want to make it clear that I am not out to convince the reader of the reality of extraterrestrials. I do not wish to change any minds, only to open a few eyes. I'll be the first to admit that these UFO stories are quite unbelievable. And I would agree that the evidence for the reality of extraterrestrial aliens is not conclusive—only suggestive. So if you decide to look down skeptically on these stories, you have every right to do so. There may very well be a psychological explanation for this material, though so far no one has made a truly convincing case for one.

What I have done here, quite simply, is taken "nonfiction" accounts of UFO entities and proceeded with the assumption— granted, a very large one—that these reported beings are what the witnesses and investigators say they are, that is, extraterrestrials. For the purposes of this book I will *assume* that these UFO-related aliens are real.

Belief actually doesn't matter. Whether you think that encounters with UFO aliens are physically real or mere hallucinations is irrelevant. We have field guides to wildlife. We have dream dictionaries. We have folklore encyclopedias. Some deal with things that are objectively real, others deal with things that are subjectively real. But whatever the nature of the reality, our knowledge of it can be organized.

With Madison Avenue appropriating aliens to sell their products, it's clear that our culture's current intense interest in all manner of things extraterrestrial has now attained corporate-level strength. So before the subject becomes warped beyond all recognition, I've decided to present this who's who to the extraterrestrial horde.

A Little History

Eyewitness reports of contact with alien beings seen in crafts descending from the sky are now at least a century old. The first apparent claim of contact with an alien craft reportedly took place on November 25, 1896. That afternoon Colonel H. G. Shaw and his companion Camille Spooner were nearly abducted by three tall creatures with large eyes who eventually departed in a cigar-shaped craft. Shaw was convinced the craft and the beings were from Mars. The story, though probably regarded as a tall tale at the time, is remarkably similar to those that appear in great abundance today, nearly a century later.

Reports of close encounters with alleged aliens continued to appear after the turn of the century. Incidents occurred in the summer of 1901 in Bournebrook, England; in 1910 in Baltimore, Maryland; in 1919 in western Australia; in 1925 in La Mancha, Spain; in 1944 in Rochester, Pennsylvania—and right on up to and after June 24,1947, when a sighting of several mysterious craft by pilot Kenneth Arnold led a newsman to label these objects "flying saucers." Within weeks of this milestone event, encounters with little men from spaceships were reported in Tennessee, Italy, and France. It should be noted that most flying saucer investigators of the time rejected these humanoid stories as just too fantastic. The flying saucer stories were already hard enough to believe; tales of UFO pilots were just beyond the pale.

By the early 1950s, the reports of encounters with spacemen

took on a wholly different look. Some people were beginning to claim close contacts with the "space brothers." These encounters were of a less fearful nature than earlier reports and also less a product of chance. And the spacemen looked different, too. They were very human, often tall, blond, and beautiful.

One of the first contactees was George Adamski, a Polish-born émigré who worked a food and drink stand on the slopes of Mount Palomar in California and took pictures of what he claimed were alien spaceships. Then on November 29, 1952, he drove out into the desert with some friends to see a spacecraft. When it arrived, Adamski had his friends wait a mile away while he went off to meet a man he claimed was from Venus.

But for his shoulder-length blond hair, the friendly Venusian looked like a regular guy. He communicated with Adamski through sign language and telepathy, preaching peace and anti-nuclear sentiments, and telling Adamski of their "mother ships" in orbit and "scout ships" that visited Earth. In the years that followed, Adamski claimed not only to have met aliens from most of the planets in the solar system but also to have visited the Moon, with its trees and rivers—all of which proved to be scientifically absurd. Dozens of other contactee tales followed Adamski's, further reducing the credibility of any stories involving alien beings and UFOs.

Yet, along with a flood of science fiction movies dealing with a variety of monsters from outer space, the close encounters continued. In fact, the entire situation took a dramatic turn in October of 1954, when a flood of credible alien contact stories emerged from France and other parts of Europe. In sharp contrast to the tall friendly space brothers, however, these aliens tended to be short and rather aggressive. A few French investigators took these reports seriously. Then in November and December another wave of entity reports emerged, this time from South America, and another handful of researchers became believers. For most of the rest of the world, however, this was still all very silly stuff.

But in the decade and a half that followed, three highly significant cases occurred that served to convince many more open-minded people that the occupant reports were not only real but potentially threatening. The first took place in Brazil in November of 1957 and involved the first abduction of a human, Antonio Villas-Boas, by aliens for apparently sexual purposes. What is significant about this episode is that the story was ignored as absurd at the time even by UFO researchers and was not written up in English until the mid-1960s. By this time a second landmark case had occurred, that of Betty and Barney Hill in New Hampshire in September of 1961. The Hill case bore many similarities to the earlier Villas-Boas story, but it, too, did not reach the press until 1965. By this time a third case, the case that some say convinced the world, had already occurred and made believers out of many former skeptics.

This landmark case, which is not included in this field guide because the description of the entity seen was not detailed enough for an artist's reconstruction, occurred in the late afternoon of April 24, 1964. A police officer named Lonnie Zamora was on patrol outside of Socorro, New Mexico, when he was distracted by a loud roaring noise and a blue tapering flame low on the horizon. When he investigated, he realized that the flame was descending into an open canyon. Suddenly the flame and noise stopped, and he saw an egg-shaped craft far enough in the distance that he thought it might be a car overturned by vandals. As he approached in his patrol car, Zamora spotted what appeared to be two "kids" beside the polished white metal object. Slightly smaller than an adult, the kids, strangely enough, were wearing white one-piece suits. Zamora then realized that things were not what they seemed.

The police officer took his eyes off the scene for a moment as he called in a possible accident on his police radio. Zamora then pulled his car to a stop and got out just as the loud roar started up again, and he saw a flame beneath the object as it rose into the sky. By the time the police chief responded to his initial call, the object had sped away and disappeared. But upon investigation, the police found that the bushes were still smoldering in the place where the object had landed. There were also four indentations in the ground, apparently marks left behind from the object's landing gear, which Zamora had seen as it took off.

The caliber of the witness was such that the police chief cordoned off the area and launched an immediate inquiry in which the FBI, CIA, and Air Force all became involved, either directly or indirectly. Other witnesses had called the police station claiming to have seen a mysterious flame or heard a deafening noise. Yet, despite a concerted effort to find an explanation for the incident, the case was never solved. It certainly was not for lack of trying. Major Hector Quintanilla, then director of the Air Force's Project Blue Book, did everything he could to solve the case, taking it all the way to the White House, but still he came up empty-handed.

By the late 1960s the reality of UFO-related entities was no longer such a taboo subject. Gradually it dawned on UFO investigators that these reports actually represented a topic of significant probative value. Many thought that a solution to the UFO mystery could come only through the investigation of these "occupant" or "entity" cases. Recognition of a sort came in 1972, when the astronomer and former advisor for the Air Force's Project Blue Book, J. Allen Hynek, coined the term "Close Encounters of the Third Kind" for claims "in which the presence of animated creatures is reported." When Steven Spielberg appropriated the term for his blockbuster movie of the same title five years later, the subject of UFO aliens would soon become deeply etched on the public mind.

The Aliens

The popular image of extraterrestrials is of short humanlike beings with lightbulb-shaped heads, almond-shaped black eyes, and fragile bodies. They are said to have an obsession with human physiology and reproduction, siphoning off sperm and ova from their human subjects, inserting nasal tracking implants, and showing off their weird hybrid babies. This image of the Grays, as they now are commonly known, took firm root in the mainstream soil of cultural consciousness with the publication of Whitley Strieber's nonfiction best-seller *Communion* in 1987. The portrait of the Grays on the cover of his book struck a chord of recognition in many people.

If the Grays are it, or more precisely *them,* why then, you might argue, do we need a field guide? Well, to begin with, although the Grays are by far the most common type of extraterrestrial now encountered, there are many variants involved. Generally speaking, the Grays are three and a half feet tall and possess the characteristic grayish white skin. They have large, hairless, fetuslike heads with narrow jaws that taper to a "V." Their black eyes have no pupils or eyelids and wrap around the head to the temple. They have no nose, just small nostril holes, and a thin, lipless slit for a mouth. Their torsos are rather scrawny; their arms and legs are long and thin. And their hands have three nontapering fingers.

But there are also reports of Grays that are five, six, or seven feet tall. Some have brown or black skin. Some have eyes with a thin nictitating membrane. Some have fine wispy hair. Some have four fingers, and others have fingers that end in suction-cup tips or claws. Some have large folds along the back of their heads, deep creases along their foreheads, or a pronounced brow ridge about the eyes. Another source of variation among the Grays, though clearly cultural, is clothing. Some wear jumpsuits or long robes. Some outfits are blue; some are not. Others appear not to wear clothes. In sum, the differences in size and appearance among the Grays may represent their origins on different planets, or it may not. There is really no way to know with the information available. The point is that there are many types of Grays.

Although we have been culturally conditioned to believe that the Grays who spirit people out of their bedrooms or cars are *the* aliens, these creatures are by no means the only type of beings encountered. There is a great diversity of UFO occupants, and I see no reason to discard one in favor of another. I don't feel that popularity is necessarily a reliable barometer of reality. Besides, there has been a tendency on the part of some investigators to ignore reports of extremely odd aliens, to ignore data that do not suit their theories. This book attempts to redress that situation, portraying extraterrestrial anatomy in all its various forms.

Either the eyewitness reports can be trusted, or they can't. If they are reliable, then the aliens certainly display a bewildering array of anatomical forms and show a great diversity of shape, size, skin color, and other features. Through the years there have been aliens of all colors: black, white, red, orange, yellow, blue, violet, and of course, gray and green. They can be minuscule, just a few inches tall, or tower above the witnesses, standing 10 feet tall or more. They range from small hairy dwarfs to bald giants. Some look nearly human, others comically alien. A few are living manifestations of a nightmare. While they often look like flesh-and-blood or metallic beings, many can perform ghostlike feats such as walking through walls. They display various eccentricities in their dress, behavior, and speech content. Some act like saints, others like demons. And when it comes to telling fibs, it has been noted, no politician on Earth could do better.

Yet, despite their variety, there is a certain consistency of description. While some aliens are reported as being mere blobs or resembling a Coke machine, the vast majority of reported aliens are described as bipeds, though there have been a few reports of unipeds as well. The presence of legs, however, does not necessarily imply their use for locomotion, as many aliens are apparently able to float in the air, at least in this world. Their legs pretty much vary as humans legs do, while the feet are usually not described in much detail, other than when they are strikingly different from our own—the disk-shaped pedestal foot of one uniped seen in Brazil comes to mind.

Almost all aliens have torsos of some kind with upper and lower limbs and a head, though there are exceptions here as well. Some apparently have no arms, others have more than two, and on rare occasions the upper limbs take the form of tentacles or wings. Mostly their arms end in hands, though not always, and when they do they often have fewer than the usual complement of fingers—three or four being most common. In a few cases, claws or strange tool-like instruments have been reported in the place of hands.

When it comes to heads, a few aliens actually don't seem to possess one. But unlike their counterparts in science fiction, none have more than one. Many aliens have larger than normal heads, the cranium often being disproportionately large, but possessing a head does not necessarily entail having a neck, if some alien descriptions can be trusted.

Though alien faces vary enormously, most follow a general human arrangement of features. Almost all have two forward-facing eyes, but a few are graced with a third or possess fewer than the standard number—one or none. Their eyes, in any case, are often larger than a human's or rounder or more slitlike, and tend to wrap further around their heads than ours. They are usually solid black and without pupils, whites, or irises. Sometimes their eyes are reported as glowing or multiple like a fly's or possessing vertical pupils. Aliens often lack a nose, having only nostrils, or else they seem to posses a particularly sharp one. Their mouths are usually small, almost always lipless, and therefore resemble a mere slit. Reports of teeth are extremely rare. Aliens' ears also rarely receive mention, either because they don't have any or because they are mere orifices. Occasionally the ears will resemble an animal's: a calf's, say, or a mouse's.

The skin of the aliens also shows great variation. The ubiquitous small humanoids known as the Grays have smooth, pale, hairless skin, which can be either pasty-looking or translucent. Often witnesses can't tell if they are seeing the aliens' naked skin or their tight-fitting clothing. This confusion can, for instance, lead an observer to describe an alien with silvery skin or clothing as a robot. The wrinkled skin of a few aliens has led witnesses to refer to this type as the "Elders." Another humanoid type has a distinctly pockmarked or ruddy skin. Reports of green-skinned aliens—literally "little green men"—are rare but not uncommon. Some animal-like aliens seem to have a scaly, reptilian skin. There are also many reports of extremely hairy aliens; often these have a more humanoid than animal form.

Who's Who?

During the past quarter century, several researchers have tried to bring some order to the perplexing variety of alien forms by creating classification systems of one kind or another. Many researchers, hoping perhaps to make the extraterrestrial hypothesis more palatable, tend to shoehorn the number of alien descriptions into a handful of general types. Typically the researcher will distinguish between just four basic types: the small humanoid, the experimental animal, the humanlike entity, and the robot. While this is a reasonable broad-brush approach to the topic, such a system fails not only to cover the entire range of alien types but also to address the dozens of small differences between the reported entities within each of these categories.

Other researchers have tried to categorize the entity reports by size. Longtime UFO researcher Richard Hall, for example, divided the alien horde into the three-to-four-foot-tall humanoids with large heads and slender bodies; the five-to-six-foot entities that resemble humans; and the giant or monster form, for those standing eight to twelve feet tall and possessing grotesque features. He also has a fourth category of nonbiological beings that includes robots and androids. But once again, this classification system fails to account for many entities—primarily the great many short humanoids that do not resemble the standard Grays.

One of the earliest, and still today most complete, attempts at a detailed classification of UFO entities came in the late 1960s from a Brazilian investigator named Jader U. Pereira. He examined more than 200 UFO occupant cases from around the world and found that nearly 96 percent of them were of human or humanoid form. Interestingly enough, Pereira chose as his primary distinguishing characteristic whether or not the entities wore a helmet or breathing apparatus. This is certainly sensible, as creatures needing such equipment to survive on Earth should be biologically quite different from those who do not.

Ultimately, however, I think this distinguishing feature does not work for one very simple reason. Most of the alleged aliens simply do not appear to need any breathing apparatus in our atmosphere. Therefore, most of the aliens would fall into a single category. Pereira, of course, was not unaware of this problem, as two-thirds of the entities in his study wore no helmet or breathing apparatus of any kind.

Realizing that the use or nonuse of a breathing apparatus was not enough of a distinguishing feature, Pereira went on to classify his aliens into a dozen types, again primarily on the basis of size. But in some categories he determined an alien type by cultural rather than somatic characteristics, a mistake I have tried to avoid in my own classification system. Pereira's Type 3, for example, were "males with long hair." Besides length of hair, other cultural characteristics inappropriate for a biological typology would include language, clothing, and any tools or objects used by the entities.

My biggest objection to Pereira's classification system, however, is that it lacked a category for anything apparently nonhuman or nonhumanoid. He grouped encounters of this kind into a noncategory he called "isolated cases" because they amounted to only a handful of cases. Although such creatures are in the minority, they are by no means rare, and I believe they deserve a category of their own.

Pereira's system was criticized by many and never really caught on with UFO researchers. Most came to think that a precise classification of alien types was an impossible task. Each being encountered seemed in some way so unique that any true typology of alien beings would need hundreds of types, subtypes, and variants to even pretend at completeness. Perhaps with this in mind, the creators of the Humanoid Catalog, better known as HUMCAT, did not even attempt to classify the entities themselves. This computer-based file of humanoid cases, begun in the early 1970s by David Webb and Ted Bloetcher, simply sorted the cases by the type of event—whether, for instance, the case involved an abduction—rather than by the appearance of the humanoids themselves. When the researchers looked at the entity descriptions, however, they found the creatures could be divided into three classes, but again the system was based primarily on height. They called the shorter ones, those three feet tall or less, dwarves or creatures in divers suits. Then came the "normals" or humanoid-type creatures who ranged from four to six feet tall. And their third category involved the relatively uncommon giant or anthropoid creatures.

But obviously, a flexible classification system of alien types according to broad "families" has its advantages. Such a system can provide a much needed overview of the alien encounter phenomenon. It can give people unfamiliar with the literature on the subject an idea of what eyewitnesses generally report, while researchers involved with the minutia of individual cases get a better view of the "forest."

The French researcher Eric Zucher realized this, and for his 1979 analysis of French entity cases he created an eight-part classification system that, unfortunately, was based largely on Pereira's work. Most recently, Linda Moulton Howe has begun an informal classification system of alien types that depends in part on size but also on hair, lack of hair, or hair color. Also worth mentioning is the attempt by Indiana folklorist Thomas Bullard to classify the alien horde based entirely on reports of abduction cases. His enormously detailed study found three general types of beings.

The most common were the humanoids, which Bullard defined as essentially human in shape and makeup "but different enough that you would notice one if you passed him on the street." This category accounted for two-thirds of the beings reported in abduction cases. Another quarter of the cases fit into a category he called "human" for those beings falling within the normal range of human variation. The remaining cases Bullard threw into a catchall category of nonhuman, nonhumanoid beings. This latter category made up less than 10 percent of the cases he examined.

I think Bullard's initial breakdown of alien types has two weaknesses. His third or catchall category—which includes robots, featureless life-forms, bigfoot-like creatures, brain-shaped entities, flying jelly bags, and buglike creatures—fails to distinguish between the biological and the mechanical. His alien typology also splits off the human look-alikes from the humanoid category, although by definition, it seems that the human is the standard bearer of the humanoid form and belongs in this category more than any other.

In any case, I think it worth noting that although the most common humanoids in Bullard's study were Grays, he concluded that "too many nonstandard descriptions [of the aliens] meet the same criteria of reliability as standard descriptions to throw away one and keep the other."

About This Guide

The cases in this field guide have been carefully selected. I did my best not to include any case I knew to be a hoax, although, human nature being what it is, there are no doubt a few of them in this guide. I also excluded, for purely practical reasons, many well-known UFO occupant cases, as most entity descriptions simply do not provide sufficient detail for their inclusion in a field guide of this kind. Witnesses either do not remember enough details of their encounters with these creatures for an artist to reconstruct what they saw, or the observers were not close enough to obtain the necessary details. It's also possible that the reporters or investigators of the incident failed to note the necessary details in their written accounts.

A few cases, surprisingly enough, provide *no* details at all of the entity observed. One is the famous case of Sonny Desvergers, the Florida scoutmaster who on August 19, 1952, walked into some woods to investigate what he thought was an airplane crash. Leaving three Boy Scouts behind in his car, Desvergers cut his way through 200 yards of palmetto thickets and came to a clearing where, upon looking up, he saw a metallic object blotting out the sky. Then, just before being hit by a fireball and blacking out, the scoutmaster saw a horrible being peering at him from the turret of the object. When asked by an investigator afterward what the being looked like, Desvergers replied, "I can't tell you!" Asked by the investigator if it was too horrible to describe, the witness replied, "Let it go at that. I don't want to talk about it." One can't help but wonder if what the scoutmaster saw more than four decades ago could be all that different— or more horrible—than some of the stranger creatures described in this field guide.

The lack of observational precision in most entity cases means that the most detailed descriptions we have of the aliens come from UFO landing reports, where the occupants of the craft were observed at close range, or even better yet from abduction reports, where the abductee by definition comes in close contact with the aliens. I have deliberately chosen cases drawn from a variety of observational situations so as not to skew the guide in favor of one kind of UFO experience or another.

I should also make clear that I never dismissed a case solely on the being's description, no matter how preposterous it seemed or how much it offended my common sense. The history of UFOlogy is littered with discarded beliefs based on such personal notions of what is and is not possible or acceptable. In the mid-1960s, when my interest in the subject developed, the premier UFO organization in the country accepted reports of strange lights in the sky but looked warily at reports of UFO "landings," and should any mention be made of "occupants," the case was automatically rejected.

Not until the late 1960s, with the publicity surrounding the Betty and Barney Hill case, did UFO organizations begin to take seriously the reports of entities, though as I've noted, these aliens had been reported in considerable numbers since the emergence of the "flying saucer" phenomenon in 1947 and even before. Now, of course, UFO organizations are interested in little else but the closest of all encounter stories—the abduction reports. Many of these are bedroom encounters with the black-eyed creatures and never even seem to involve a UFO or flying saucer. The craft have become superfluous.

But the presence of a craft in relation to an alien entity is essential to this field guide. There are innumerable reports of strange entities, some of which are seen the *same day* as a UFO is spotted or *in the area* of recent UFO activity, but these were not included in this volume. Unless there was a direct connection to a UFO of some sort, the entity report was excluded from this guide. As far as I'm concerned, unless the entity is described as emerging from, seen in, or at least in very close physical or temporal proximity to a strange unidentified object, the already slim chance of that entity being extraterrestrial becomes just too vanishingly small. It seems to me that without a craft of some sort, the observed being might just as well be a ghost, fairy, demon, or some other kind of occult, electromagnetic, or mental creation.

For this reason I have also chosen to exclude reports of the mysterious Men in Black who have been known to harass some UFO witnesses after their sightings. The Men in Black are usually described as tall humans in black suits but with something not quite right about them. Their skin may be of a corpselike pallor, or their eyes may be in some sense unusual, or their voice may seem mechanical. In any case, while some researchers believe these are government agents, others think the MIB, as they are commonly known, are extraterrestrials in human disguise. But with only one questionable exception I know of, the MIB are never seen in conjunction with a UFO.

My proposed classification scheme for the alien horde does not pretend to be scientific. I am not trying to lay out the basis of an extraterrestrial anthropology. I'm simply trying to establish a typology of creatures that are reported to be of an extraterrestrial nature. It's really the best anyone can do considering the eyewitnesses are not biologists and the information they provide might have been distorted by errors of perception and belief, by the state of consciousness or situation they experienced, or by the investigators and reporters who have drawn the details of their experiences out of them.

I have not been able to classify the observed aliens into species, families, or such, as we know nothing or next to nothing about their genetic makeup or their breeding capabilities. And without actual specimens to examine, it is impossible to assign these creatures to any true taxonomic classification system. To make matters worse, I have never seen an extraterrestrial and neither has my illustrator. Nor have most scientists, I might add.

So how does one describe creatures whose existence is not only not recognized by science but vehemently denied? Well, you go with what you've got, and what you've got is a plethora of anecdotal reports. And then you make the best of them. The problem is that, for the most part, the physical descriptions of extraterrestrials differ substantially from one eyewitness to the next. Yet after examining dozens of such cases, hundreds actually, I have found that the entities reported fall naturally into a few broad categories that help to bring some much needed order to the bewildering variety of alien reports.

The Classification System

My classification system is based strictly on how the aliens look, on their phenotype: in other words, the observable physical characteristics of these creatures. On this basis I have been able to distinguish four reasonably separate **CLASSES** of aliens. These constitute the broadest possible categories of this alien typology. But within each of these major classes, I further found several different **TYPES** of entities. And since there was still considerable variation within each of these types, I needed to further subdivide the alien types into **VARIANTS.** These variants are drawn from specific cases and constitute the descriptive events that form the heart of this field guide.

The first, and by far the largest, class of aliens is the **HUMANOID.** This class is reserved for those extraterrestrials who exhibit the same basic body plan as the human: They have a cylindrical trunk surmounted by a head with two arms and two legs attached at the shoulders and hips, respectively. When the aliens were more animal than human, I placed them into a second class that I call **ANIMALIAN.** This includes anything that's hairy, scaly, moves on four legs, or has wings. The third class of aliens exhibited a mechanical nature that could best be called **ROBOTIC.** Though a robotlike walk would not be sufficient to place an entity in this category, a square head would. The fourth class of aliens I call **EXOTIC.** This tends to be a catchall class and includes any entity that is nonhumanoid, nonanimalian, and nonrobotic.

Within the class of humanoids, I then distinguished five types of entities. The first type, the **"HUMAN,"** includes all alleged extraterrestrials who would be indistinguishable in a crowd of people on, let's say, the streets of Manhattan, but are reported in the vicinity of, emerging from, or seen in a UFO. These alleged aliens are all but indistinguishable from ordinary humans. However, these extraterrestrials should not be confused with actual humans that UFO abductees often report being on board the craft with them.

Among these human look-alikes, I found six major variants. The most prevalent are the six feet and taller, blue-eyed "beautiful people," often with shoulder-length blond hair. They are commonly referred to in the UFO literature as "Nordics." Another variant are the extraterrestrials who resemble humans but who apparently require a space suit and helmet of some kind in our world. Then there are the human-looking entities with highly wrinkled faces who are often referred to as "Elders." Three other less common variants are also noted.

The second major type of humanoids are **SHORT GRAYS.** I have given these entities their own type simply because there are so many reports of encounters with them. But, as I've already pointed out, even within this popular type there are noticeable variants. Some require helmets or some type of breathing apparatus, for instance, while others have a slightly more insectoid-looking face than your standard off-the-UFO Gray.

Short humanoids that did not fit the standard Gray mold

constitute the third major type of humanoids. I call this type **SHORT NON-GRAYS.** Variants here include actual "little green men"; short humanoids with pitted faces, of which there have been quite a few reports; an extremely hairy short humanoid who notably seemed more human than animal; as well as some three-inch-high entities that, despite their stature, were also clearly humanoid.

Extremely tall or **GIANT** entities are the fourth type of humanoid. One variant here is a ten-foot being with three eyes; another is a cyclops. Humanoids with the standard complement of eyes but standing more than 8 feet tall are also included in this alien type.

The fifth type of humanoid, which I call **NONCLASSIC,** is a catchall for all remaining humanoids. The variants here include a solid black form, a mummylike being, and an entity with no hands, among others.

The second class of aliens, animalian, consists of five distinct types of aliens. It should be noted, however, that despite their animal-like appearance, the behavior and demeanor of these aliens is usually more human than animal.

The first of these types, **HAIRY MAMALIAN,** distinguishes itself from the humanoids by hair that covers the creature's entire body, or at least all that is visible of it. These may be tall bigfoot-like creatures, animals with four legs, or entities with batlike faces.

The second type, **REPTILIAN,** includes green, scaly entities with snoutlike faces and large oval eyes, silvery goblins, and swamp-type creatures. The type name refers only to the creature's hairless skin and general appearance.

The third type, **AMPHIBIAN,** is reserved for froglike entities. This type name refers only to the creatures' smooth skin and has nothing to do, at least as far as I'm aware, with matters aquatic.

The fourth type is **INSECTOID** and includes all insectlike beings with long spindly limbs and large multifaceted eyes. Variants of this type include any creature with rounded wings, which others may call fairies, as well as those resembling a grasshopper or praying mantis.

The fifth type in the animalian class is the **AVIAN.** These are simply creatures with birdlike wings. There are few reports of this type and only a single variety is noted.

In the robotic class I distinguish between two types of aliens. The first is the **METALLIC,** consisting of robots that look entirely like tin cans or slabs of metal. The second type of robot I call **FLESHY,** and by this I mean androidlike beings that display features of living beings either human or animal. Robots with either humanlike arms or legs, for instance, or displaying in part the scaly skin of a reptile would be entities of the fleshy robotic type.

The fourth class of aliens I call exotic. These come in two types. One is the **APPARITIONAL** and includes ghostlike entities and nonhumanoid creatures that are only partially formed and look as if they exist at least in part in another dimension. The other exotic type I term **PHYSICAL.** This is really a catchall category and includes such variants as an entity in the shape of a brain and a bloblike thing.

This alien classification system is meant as a general guideline only. The classes, types, and variants are not intended to be straitjackets. Some entities could be placed in more than one of these categories. There are obviously many transitional forms, humanoids that act like robots and hairy humanoids that resemble animals, for instance. I am amenable to making category adjustments in future editions of this volume, given additional information on any single descriptive case or suggestions for a better, more encompassing, more accurate extraterrestrial typology.

Classification Table

CLASS	TYPE	VARIANT
Humanoid	"Human"	6
Humanoid	Short Gray	3
Humanoid	Short Non-Gray	8
Humanoid	Giant	4
Humanoid	Nonclassic	4
Animalian	Hairy Mammalian	5
Animalian	Reptilian	3
Animalian	Amphibian	2
Animalian	Insectoid	2
Animalian	Avian	1
Robotic	Metallic	3
Robotic	Fleshy	4
Exotic	Physical	2
Exotic	Apparitional	2

HUMANOID

CLASS: *Humanoid*
TYPE: *"Human"*
VARIANT: *1, aka "Nordic"*
DISTINGUISHING CHARACTERISTIC: *blond hair*

DESCRIPTIVE INCIDENT
DATE: *Summer 1975*
LOCATION: *La Junta, Colorado*
WITNESS: *Jamie W.*

At about eight o'clock in the morning the sky was vivid blue with not a cloud in sight. Jamie W. and husband were driving their Volkswagen from Boulder back to Lamar, Colorado, where they lived. No one else was on the highway. Suddenly they saw something off to the left of the road. About 350 feet up in the air was an elongated donut-shaped object—they could actually see the sky through the center of it. Its size was on the order of half a football field, and it had a highly polished metallic look.

The couple pulled their car over to the side of the road but couldn't get any closer to the object because of a barbed-wire fence. They sat there watching it for 30 to 45 minutes. Jamie got the impression that whatever they were watching was watching them back. So she mentally greeted them, saying, "My name is Jamie. Welcome to our planet." Then suddenly three or four little white clouds popped in from the east, traveling west, followed by a huge cloud that moved in front of and covered the metallic object. When this cloud moved on, the object with a hole in the center was gone. They then started the car and resumed their trip to Lamar, but strangely, Jamie, who was normally hyperactive, now felt unusually calm and peaceful.

Years later, during a hypnosis session, Jamie revealed that as soon as she had seen the object she had wanted to run to it. Though her husband had told her to stay in the car, she remembered suddenly being inside the object, where she was greeted by two beings, one male, the other female. They looked very "Scandinavian." They were tall, about six and a half feet, thin, and beautiful. Their hair was long and blond and so were their eyelashes. Jamie noted that their skin was so white it was almost translucent. Both wore blue jumpsuits. The male entity wore a silver belt.

Jamie did not want to leave the ship but was told that she must go back. Suddenly she found herself in the car again, determined to pass on their message of peace.

SOURCE: *Interview by the author, July 10, 1987. Laramie, Wyoming.*

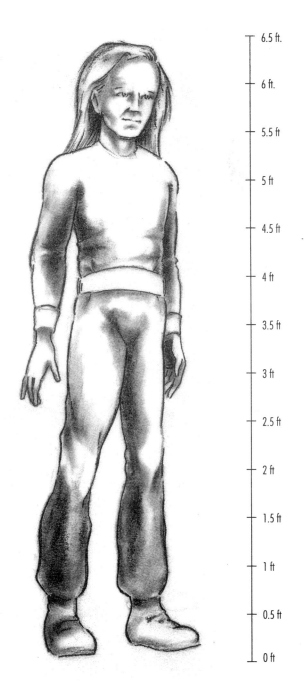

6.5 ft.

6 ft.

5.5 ft

5 ft

4.5 ft

4 ft

3.5 ft

3 ft

2.5 ft

2 ft

1.5 ft

1 ft

0.5 ft

0 ft

CLASS: *Humanoid*
TYPE: *"Human"*
VARIANT: *2, aka "Elder"*
DISTINGUISHING CHARACTERISTIC: *wrinkled face*

DESCRIPTIVE INCIDENT
DATE: *December 3, 1967*
LOCATION: *Ashland, Nebraska*
WITNESS: *Herbert Schirmer*

At 2:30 A.M. on a clear moonless night, after investigating a report of a livestock disturbance, state trooper, Herbert Schirmer approached what he thought were the red lights of a truck on the highway. On closer inspection the truck turned out to be a hovering metallic saucer-shaped object with red lit portholes around its rim. A catwalk surrounded the object. Schirmer then saw the craft rise, fluttering from side to side and emitting a fiery glow from its underside.

At 3:00 A.M. Schirmer returned to his office and noted in the log that he had seen a flying saucer. He could not account for about 20 minutes of lost time. Later that night he found a red welt on his neck. Schirmer also began complaining of fierce headaches and a buzzing in his head that disturbed his sleep. Eventually he quit his job.

Under hypnosis more details of the episode emerged. Schirmer recalled that in the presence of the object his car engine, lights, and radio had all failed. When strange beings approached his patrol car, Schirmer found himself unable to use his gun. A green gas enveloped his car, and he passed out. When he came to, one of the beings, apparently the leader, invited him into the craft.

This humanoid had a stern appearance. He stood about five feet tall. He had a long thin head with a noticeably wrinkled forehead. His eyes were of normal size, as were his mouth, nose, and eyebrows, but the pupils were enlarged and elongated. He had gray white skin and seemed to be wearing a uniform with boots and gloves. On the right breast of the uniform was a patch bearing a winged serpent. A tight-fitting dark hood covered his head. Over the left ear was a small round device with a two-inch-long antenna.

The leader, who asked if Schirmer was the "watchman of the area," offered to show the patrolman how their equipment worked. Inside the craft, in a room measuring about 20 by 26 feet and six feet high, the witness was shown the engine, a crystalline rotor linked to two columns. The leader then conversed with Schirmer and explained that they came from another galaxy but had bases on other planets in the solar system. They were contacting earthlings to prepare them for eventual open contact, to prevent them from destroying Earth, and also to confuse them.

Schirmer was then led back to his patrol car and told to forget the experience. This story was the only abduction episode investigated by the Condon Committee, the official UFO study funded by the U.S. Air Force and conducted at the University of Colorado in the late 1960s.

SOURCE: *Ralph and Judy Blum,* Beyond Earth: Man's Contact with UFOs *(New York: Bantam, 1974).*

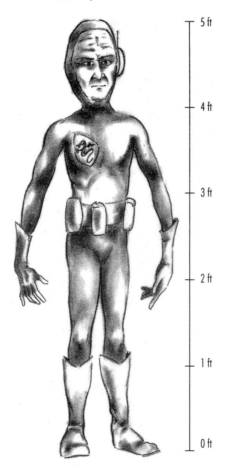

CLASS: *Humanoid*	**DESCRIPTIVE INCIDENT**
TYPE: *"Human"*	**DATE:** *July 4, 1947*
VARIANT: *3*	**LOCATION:** *Roswell, New Mexico*
DISTINGUISHING CHARACTERISTIC:	**WITNESSES:** *W. Curry Holden,*
bald head	*an unnamed nurse, and others*

At 11:30 P.M. on a stormy Fourth of July more than a half dozen people saw a bright object roar overhead. Some thought it might be a meteor or a disabled aircraft. A team of archaeologists headed by W. Curry Holden watched it fall to the ground. The next morning they were the first to stumble upon the site of the crash. The object, which was embedded in the side of a desert cliff, looked like a crashed airplane without wings. Near the wreckage they found three bodies. One was visible through the hole in the side of the craft; the other two were outside it. Two other men who happened to have camped nearby also came across the bodies, which they said were no more than four or five feet tall. The military then quickly cordoned off the area, and the witnesses were sworn to secrecy.

But almost a half century later, the whole bizarre story would emerge nonetheless, including the testimony of Glen Dennis, who had been the mortician at Ballard's Funeral Home in Roswell. On July 5, Dennis was summoned to pick up an injured airman and bring him to the hospital. After delivering the airman to the emergency room, Dennis headed to the hospital lounge for a drink. As he walked down the corridor, one of the nurses saw him and asked, "How did you get in here?" She told him he should get out before he got into trouble. Later he was spotted by an Army officer who summoned two MPs to escort him out.

A few days later Dennis arranged to meet the nurse in private to ask her what all the fuss had been about. After swearing him to secrecy, she told him that on the day in question she had been asked to assist two doctors whom she had never seen before. Upon entering a foul-smelling room, she found the doctors examining three "foreign bodies," two of which were very badly mutilated.

She described their anatomy as follows: Their heads were larger than a human's and were apparently bald. Their eyes were small and sunken, and their noses were concave with two small openings. They had no ears, just holes on the side of the head with tiny lobes. Their mouths were lipless and thin. And instead of teeth, they had what looked like rawhide strips in their mouths.

She didn't notice any clothes. But she was struck by their arms. Unlike human arms, the distance between their wrist and elbow was greater than between their elbow and shoulder. She saw only four long slender fingers on their hands. And the ends of their fingers had little hollow pads that looked like suction cups.

Feeling nauseous, the nurse finally left the examination room. Soon after, the doctors exited as well. After hearing this story, the mortician never saw the nurse again. Though the details of this case vary somewhat from witness to witness, including the descriptions of the aliens, it is viewed by many UFO researchers as perhaps the most important UFO case of all time.

SOURCE: *Kevin D. Randle and Donald R. Schmitt,* The Truth About the UFO Crash at Roswell *(New York: M. Evans, 1994).*

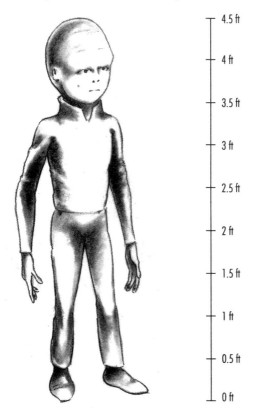

CLASS: *Humanoid*	DESCRIPTIVE INCIDENT
TYPE: *"Human"*	DATE: *November 1, 1954*
VARIANT: *4*	LOCATION: *Cennina, Arezzo, Italy*
DISTINGUISHING CHARACTERISTIC:	WITNESS: *Rosa Lotti*
teeth	

On the morning of All Saints' Day, this respectable 40-year-old peasant woman and mother of four got up at 6:30 to go to church. Carrying a bouquet of carnations, as well as her shoes and stockings so as not to soil them, Lotti was passing through some woods when she saw a strange object in a grassy clearing. The object was spindle-shaped, somewhat like two cones sharing a common base. It measured about six feet high and three feet wide and seemed to be covered with a metal the color of leather. Inside the lower half, through an open glass door, Lotti could see two small seats and controls.

Lotti stopped in her tracks when two little men appeared from behind the object. Though they were only about three feet tall, they were otherwise perfectly human in appearance. Despite their childlike size, however, their faces were those of older men, though clean shaven. The beings seemed cheerful and had short protruding white teeth. Their overalls, doublets, and cloaks were gray, and their helmets were like leather.

The two midgets spoke to her in words she could not understand. Then suddenly they grabbed her flowers and stockings and placed the stolen goods in their rocket. One being then pointed a tubelike device at her, as if to take her picture. Frightened, Lotti began running away, but at a turn in the path she glanced back and saw the two beings still standing by their craft.

When she got to church, she recounted the episode to the parish priest and later to the police. It was the priest who associated the craft with *"dischi volanti"* and the creatures with *"i Marziani."* Later nine other witnesses who had seen the object came forward, including two young boys who reported having seen it and a lady "chatting with the men."

SOURCE: *Sergio Conti, "The Cennina Landing,"* Flying Saucer Review *18, no. 5 (September-October 1972): pp. 11–15.*

3 ft

2 ft

1 ft

0 ft

CLASS: *Humanoid*
TYPE: *"Human"*
VARIANT: *5, aka "Easter Island" head*
DISTINGUISHING CHARACTERISTIC:
long chin

DESCRIPTIVE INCIDENT
DATE: *August 28, 1972*
LOCATION: *Bahía Blanca, Buenos Aires, Argentina*
WITNESS: *Eduardo Fernando Dedeu*

It was 3:00 A.M. and the witness, a car mechanic, was driving home in an old car when he stopped to fix the car's malfunctioning radio antenna. That's when he first noticed the hitchhiker by the side of the road and gave the man a lift. Dedeu tried conversing with his passenger but gave up when the man's only replies were incomprehensible sounds.

The strange hitchhiker was a little more than six feet tall and wore a caplike hat and a coat with its collar turned up. He looked human except for his head, which resembled those of the statues on Easter Island. His long chin seemed almost to reach the middle of his chest.

After about 15 miles, the car suddenly lost power and its lights went out. Dedeu then saw what appeared to be a big luminous bus overturned on the highway ahead. When he stopped the car and got out to get a better look, he realized the "bus" was a UFO. The object, which was actually moving over a field, had white lights in its windows and a green light underneath.

By the time Dedeu turned around and got back in the car, however, the hitchhiker was gone. The passenger-side door was open, and its handle was wrenched off and lying on the floor. With the object gone, the car now started properly, and Dedeu drove around trying to find his passenger, but without success. A nearby night watchman later confirmed the presence of a mysterious light hovering over the area.

Humanoids fitting this same long-chinned description were seen repeatedly in connection with UFOs over the seven-month period that followed in Argentina, and as recently as September 1994 in the United States.

SOURCE: *Jane Thomas, "The Hitch-Hiker from Space,"* Flying Saucer Review 18, no. 6 (November-December 1972): pp 23–24; and "Further Details about the 'Hitch-Hiker' from Space," Flying Saucer Review Case Histories, *supp. 14 (April 1973): p. iii.*

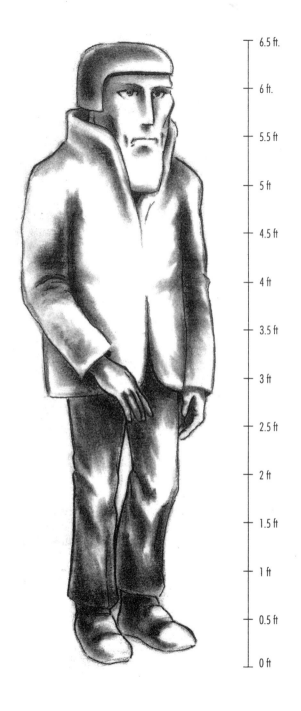

6.5 ft.

6 ft.

5.5 ft

5 ft

4.5 ft

4 ft

3.5 ft

3 ft

2.5 ft

2 ft

1.5 ft

1 ft

0.5 ft

0 ft

CLASS: *Humanoid*	DESCRIPTIVE INCIDENT
TYPE: *"Human"*	DATE: *October 15, 1957*
VARIANT: *6*	LOCATION: *São Francisco de Sales,*
DISTINGUISHING CHARACTERISTIC:	*Minas Gerais, Brazil*
space suit	WITNESSES: *Antonio Villas-Boas*

On two previous evenings Villas-Boas, a 23-year-old farmer, and his brother had observed a strange light over their farm. Then, at 1:00 A.M. on this cold, clear, and starry night, Villas-Boas saw a red star that grew to a bright egg-shaped object with a rotating cupola. The object, which measured 35 feet long by about 23 feet wide, first hovered over his tractor. But as the object landed nearby on its tripod legs, the tractor engine died. Frightened, Villas-Boas quickly jumped off but was grabbed before he had run but a couple of steps. Four beings then struggled with him and took him aboard the craft.

The beings were about five feet tall. They wore a very tight-fitting suit made of a soft, thick, unevenly striped gray material that seemed to continue at the extremities as gloves and thick-soled shoes. The garment reached up to the neck, where it was connected to a helmet that hid everything except the beings' small light-blue eyes visible through lenslike windows. Three tubes emerged from the top of their tall helmets and ran down to their ribs, where the tubes entered the clothing. Their uniform included a belt with breast strap as well as a breast badge or shield.

After communicating among themselves in slowly emitted growls, the beings began to forcibly undress Villas-Boas. They then washed his body with something like a soft moist sponge that spread a clear thick liquid over his body. He was then led into another room through a door that was inscribed with strange lettering. He waited a long time in this room and became nauseous because of a sickening smoke that was pumped into it.

Finally the door opened and a naked woman walked in. She had blond hair parted in the middle and blue eyes that were longer than they were wide and slanted outward. She had a straight nose, high cheeks, a pointed chin, and a wide face. Her lips were thin and her ears were small. She measured only about four feet five inches tall. It is assumed that, under their space suits, the other beings would have a similar humanlike appearance.

The woman embraced Villas-Boas, making clear exactly what she desired. He obliged. Afterward the space-suited beings came in and departed with the woman. But before she left she pointed to her belly, smiled, and pointed at the sky. When his clothes were brought in, Villas-Boas dressed and was given a tour of the craft. Afterward the beings showed him a metal ladder and signaled that he go down it. Villas-Boas observed the craft take off. It was 5:30 in the morning.

SOURCE: *Coral and Jim Lorenzen,* Flying Saucer Occupants *(New York: Signet, 1967).*

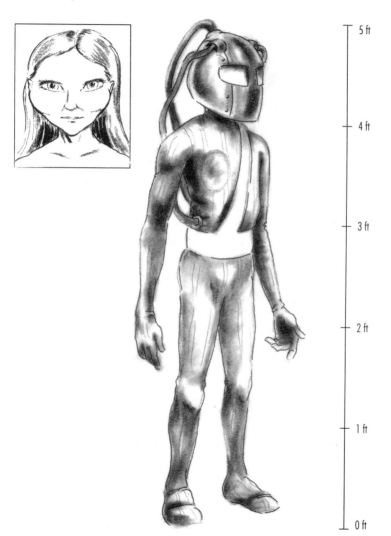

CLASS: *Humanoid*
TYPE: *Short Gray*
VARIANT: *1, Classic*
DISTINGUISHING CHARACTERISTIC:
black, wrap-around eyes

DESCRIPTIVE INCIDENT
DATE: *September 19, 1961*
LOCATION: *Lancaster, New Hampshire*
WITNESSES: *Betty and Barney Hill*

Returning from a vacation in Canada, the Hills were headed south on U.S. Route 3 when they spotted a bright starlike object on an erratic course. Barney, a black 39-year-old postal worker, and Betty, a white 41-year-old social worker, stopped their car several times in the course of the evening to look at the object through binoculars. At one point the object swung around in front of their car and hovered just a few hundred feet above the ground. Through binoculars Barney saw windows along the side of the glowing pancake-shaped object. When it tilted, he could make out through the portholes a half-dozen figures working in the illuminated interior. They appeared to be wearing black uniforms with billed caps.

Now hysterical, Barney dashed back to the car and sped off down the highway. The Hills then heard a series of beeps, felt the car vibrating, and were overwhelmed by a feeling of drowsiness. When the couple reached their home in Portsmouth, New Hampshire, it was more two hours later than it should have been—which, along with a circle of warts that appeared around Barney's groin, worried them immensely. Betty soon began suffering from terrifying dreams of a UFO experience. Two years later they sought the help of a Boston psychiatrist, who hypnotized them and elicited a bizarre story.

The Hills recounted turning off the highway and being approached by a group of "men" in the road. Betty's and Barney's descriptions of the beings varied slightly. They agreed that the beings were small, about five feet tall, and had broad foreheads and round faces that tapered toward the chin. In her dream Betty remembered large noses and black hair, but Barney recalled no noses, just two slits for nostrils, and no hair. Under hypnosis Barney described their eyes as large and extending to the side of their face. His best recollection of a mouth was a small horizontal line, lips without muscle, which parted slightly when the beings conversed. Betty remembered that they were dressed in a uniform consisting of trousers and short jackets without zippers or buttons, and low, slip-on boots. Barney recalled that the leader wore a cap and black scarf over the shoulder.

These men led the Hills out of the car, floated them up the ramp of the waiting craft, and ushered them into a room where each underwent a type of medical examination. They took samples of Betty's skin and inserted a long needle into her navel. When she asked them where they came from, the being she thought was the leader showed her an oblong map depicting stars and explained that the lines connecting them represented trade routes. An amateur astronomer later speculated that Betty's reconstruction of this map seemed to correspond to the stars of Zeta Reticulii.

The Hills were told to forget what they had seen and then led back to their car to continue their journey. This was the first UFO abduction case to get widespread publicity.

SOURCE: *John G. Fuller,* The Interrupted Journey *(New York: Dial Press, 1966).*

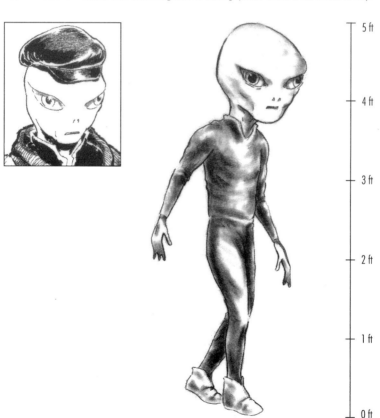

CLASS: *Humanoid*	DESCRIPTIVE INCIDENT
TYPE: *Short Gray*	DATE: *August 26, 1972*
VARIANT: *2*	LOCATION: *Allagash Waterway,*
DISTINGUISHING CHARACTERISTIC:	*Maine*
turtlelike lower half of face	WITNESSES: *Jim and Jack Weiner,*
	Charlie Fotz, and Chuck Rak

On the fifth day of their canoe trip in northern Maine, the Weiner twins and their two friends decided to replenish their scarce food supply by doing a little night fishing on Eagle Lake. Before sliding their canoe off into the water, they prepared a large bonfire, good for a couple of hours, so they could find their way back to camp in the pitch-dark wilderness.

The four were halfway across a cove in their canoe when they saw a silent, large bright sphere of colored light at treetop level about 200 yards away. When the object emitted a hollow blue beam onto the water and began moving toward them, the men paddled frantically for shore. Next they remembered being onshore. Though the entire episode seemed to have lasted just 15 minutes, they found their bonfire in coals.

The four men had no memory of what had happened to them, but later, under hypnosis, each independently elicited a strangely congruent testimony about being plucked from the water by the beam of light, being taken into a circular room aboard the craft, being naked and spoken to telepathically, and being forced to undergo medication examinations, including the taking of sperm samples, by alien beings. Each of the four men recalled seeing the other three on board the craft.

Jack Weiner described the beings as about five feet tall and thin. They had big egg-shaped eyes on the side of their large round heads. They had no noses, and their mouths were on the bottom, like a turtle's. Their hands had four fingerlike digits. They wore shiny coveralls similar to ski suits, but without buttons, wrinkles, or seams.

Through further hypnosis the investigator learned that the witnesses also recalled having either previous or subsequent UFO alien encounters. Odd scoop marks and scars were found on the men, and some suffered subsequent sleep and neurological problems that appeared to be related to their encounters.

SOURCE: *Raymond E. Fowler,* The Allagash Abductions, *(Tigard, Oregon: Wild Flower, 1993).*

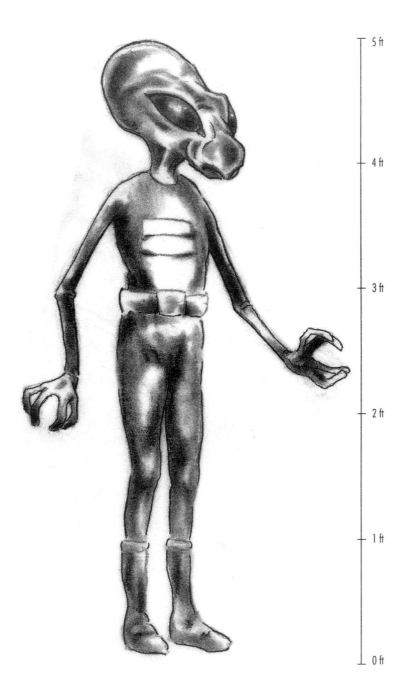

5 ft

4 ft

3 ft

2 ft

1 ft

0 ft

CLASS: *Humanoid*
TYPE: *Short Gray*
VARIANT: *3*
DISTINGUISHING CHARACTERISTIC:
helmet and "fly" eyes

DESCRIPTIVE INCIDENT
DATE: *May 15, 1951*
LOCATION: *Salzburg, Austria*
WITNESS: *Anonymous*

Leaving work at 11:00 P.M., a soldier with the U.S. Army occupation forces in Austria was walking home when a strange being stepped from behind the bushes and paralyzed him with a pencil-shaped device that made a clicking sound.

The entity, who was shorter than the soldier, had white skin and wore a dull silvery suit with a transparent helmet. The being's torso was shaped like a tin can, his legs were proportionate, but his arms were shorter than a human's and ended in three long fingers. His large-skulled head was cylindrical, hairless, and featured a very high forehead. The eyes were large and compound like those of a fly, while the ears and nose were just holes, and the mouth a mere slit.

The entity then strapped a square black plate across the soldier's chest, which made him light and enabled the humanoid to pull him effortlessly to a large landed craft, a round object 150 feet in diameter, in a nearby field. The soldier was floated to the top of the craft, where a door opened, and they entered the dark interior.

Since the craft's walls were transparent, the soldier was able to see the stars once the craft took off. They passed the Moon and flew on to a planet the soldier assumed was Mars. There the craft landed on a platform above a field that was occupied by many other saucer-shaped vehicles. As the humanoid got out and floated to the ground, the soldier noticed similar beings about and two craft containing human beings who did not acknowledge his presence.

When the entity returned, they took off and returned to Earth. The soldier was taken out the same way he had been brought in, using the pencil-shaped device and square black plate. The being then clicked the device at the soldier, removed the plate from his chest, and departed in his craft. The soldier rushed home and noticed he had been gone one hour.

In December of 1957, the soldier, seeking to unburden himself of the haunting experience, walked into the offices of *The Citizen*—a Prince George, British Columbia, newspaper—and related the details to a newsman. The newsman, who found the soldier forthright, even tried a few trick questions but failed to elicit any contradictions in the soldier's story. The being he encountered and the otherworldly trip the soldier experienced are startlingly similar to accounts that would attain prominence more than a decade later.

SOURCE: *Charles Bowen, "Fantasy or Truth? A New Look at an Old Contact Claim,"* Flying Saucer Review *13, no. 4 (July-August 1967): pp. 11–14.*

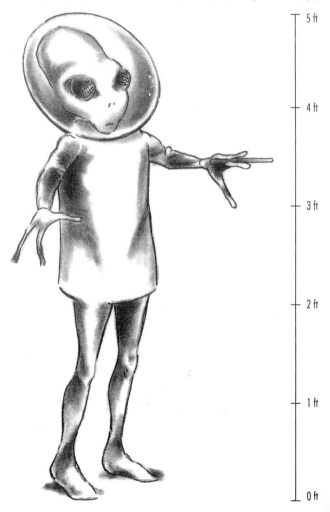

CLASS: *Humanoid*	DESCRIPTIVE INCIDENT
TYPE: *Short Non-Gray*	DATE: *November 2, 1967*
VARIANT: *1*	LOCATION: *Ririe, Idaho*
DISTINGUISHING CHARACTERISTIC:	WITNESSES: *Guy Tossie and*
scarred face	*Will Begay*

A sudden blinding flash in front of their car surprised two Navajo Indian youths on a highway just outside of Ririe at 9:30 at night. The flash was followed by the abrupt appearance of an eight-foot-wide domed saucer with flashing green and orange lights around its rim. The car stopped as the object hovered about five feet above the road, bathing the area in a green light.

Through the transparent dome, the witnesses could see two small occupants. When the dome opened, one figure floated down to the ground. It stood about three and a half feet tall and had a kind of backpack that protruded behind its hairless head. Its oval face was heavily pitted and creased, its ears were large and high, its eyes were small and round, and its mouth was slit-like. No nose was visible on the deeply scarred face.

The entity approached the car and opened the driver's-side door. When it slid behind the wheel, the two youths moved over to the right. Then, with the object in a fixed position a few feet in front, the car was driven or towed well out into a wheat field. When the car stopped, Tossie opened the door and ran to a farmhouse a quarter mile away. A bright light, apparently from the second occupant, followed him. Begay, meanwhile, cowered in the front seat as the entity spoke to him in unintelligible birdlike sounds. When the second entity returned to the car, the first emerged and the two then floated up into the object, which rose out of sight in zigzag fashion.

Tossie was so frightened that he had difficulty telling the farmer and his family the story. When they finally accompanied him back to the field, they found Begay in shock, sitting speechless in the car with his eyes closed. The car lights were on, and the engine was running. The youths reported the incident to the deputy sheriff, and the state police investigated. Others had apparently seen lights in the area, and some farmers reported that their cattle had bolted during the evening for unknown reasons.

SOURCE: *Richard Hall, Ted Bloecher, and Isabel Davis,* UFOs: A New Look *(Washington, D.C.: NICAP, 1969).*

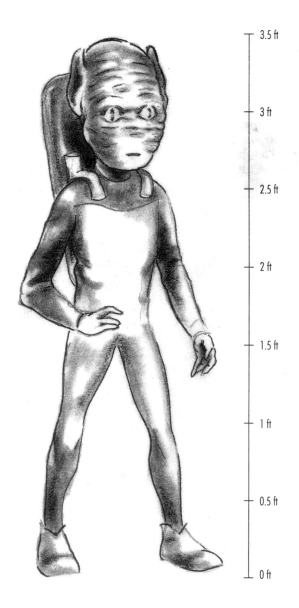

3.5 ft

3 ft

2.5 ft

2 ft

1.5 ft

1 ft

0.5 ft

0 ft

CLASS: *Humanoid*	**DESCRIPTIVE INCIDENT**
TYPE: *Short Non-Gray*	**DATE:** *August 14, 1947*
VARIANT: *2, aka "Green Man"*	**LOCATION:** *Villa Santina, Italy*
DISTINGUISHING CHARACTERISTIC:	**WITNESS:** *Rapuzzi Johannis*
green skin color	

The witness was an avid geologist. One morning, while studying unusual rock formations in Friuli in the north of Italy, he came upon a strange red object, about 30 feet wide and 18 feet high, on the rocky riverbank some 50 yards away. The lens-shaped object had a low central cupola with a telescoping antenna on top.

As the professor approached the object, he noticed what appeared to be "two boys" nearby. But upon closer examination he realized that the two boys were strange figures about three feet high. They wore dark blue translucent overalls with collars, leg cuffs, and wide belts all in red. Their heads were larger than a human's and a tight-fitting brown cap topped their hairless heads. Their faces were green skinned. They had long straight noses and fishlike slit mouths that kept opening and closing. Their yellow-green eyes were large, hemispherical, and protruding. Their pupils were vertical. They had no eyebrows or eyelashes but ringlike lids at the base of their eyes.

Overcoming his fear, the professor shouted out to them, asking who they were and where they came from. As he did so he raised his alpinist's pick, which the creatures probably interpreted as a threatening gesture. One of the two put his right hand to his belt, which then emitted a puff of smoke. Suddenly the pick flew out of the professor's hand, and he found himself down on the ground and paralyzed. The two beings then approached within six feet or so of Johannis and retrieved the pick. The professor, though paralyzed, noted that their green "hands," or claws, actually, had eight jointless digits, four opposable to the other four. He also noticed that their chests quivered, like a dog's after a long run.

As Johannis struggled to sit up, the occupants returned to their craft, climbed into it, and promptly flew away. The professor later inquired and learned that two people in the nearby village had also seen a red object climbing up into the sky.

SOURCE: *Hans Holzer,* The Ufonauts *(New York: Fawcett, 1976).*

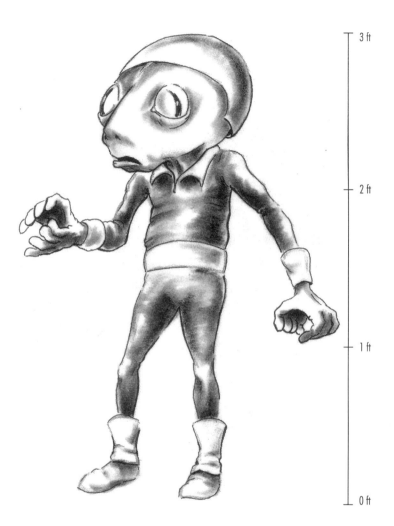

3 ft

2 ft

1 ft

0 ft

CLASS: *Humanoid*	**DESCRIPTIVE INCIDENT**
TYPE: *Short Non-Gray*	**DATE:** *July 31, 1968*
VARIANT: *3, aka "Michelin Man"*	**LOCATION:** *La Plaine des Cafres,*
DISTINGUISHING CHARACTERISTIC:	*Réunion Island (Indian Ocean)*
space suit	**WITNESS:** *Luce Fontaine*

The 31-year-old farmer, regarded as hard-working and trustworthy, was picking some grass for his rabbits in the middle of a clearing of a forest of acadia trees. Suddenly he saw an oval object suspended about 80 feet away from him. It resembled two white saucers, shining like aluminum, placed face-to-face. Though the ends of the object were dark blue, its center was transparent. Two large shiny glasslike "pedestals" were attached to this object, one above, the other below. The lower pedestal may have been resting on the ground.

The witness saw two individuals in the craft's transparent center cabin. They stood about three feet tall and were dressed head to foot in a one-piece outfit resembling the one worn by the "Michelin man." When the beings turned toward him, the witness saw their faces, which were partly masked by some kind of a helmet.

Fontaine then saw a flash, like the electric arc of a welding machine, and everything went white around him. A blast of heat and wind followed, and suddenly everything was gone. The police conducted an investigation and 10 days later found some radioactivity within 15 feet of the site of the near-landing as well as on the clothes Fontaine had worn on the day of the encounter.

SOURCE: *Gordon Creighton (trans.), "Contact Casualty on Réunion,"* Flying Saucer Review *15, no. 1, (January-February 1969): pp. 8, 11.*

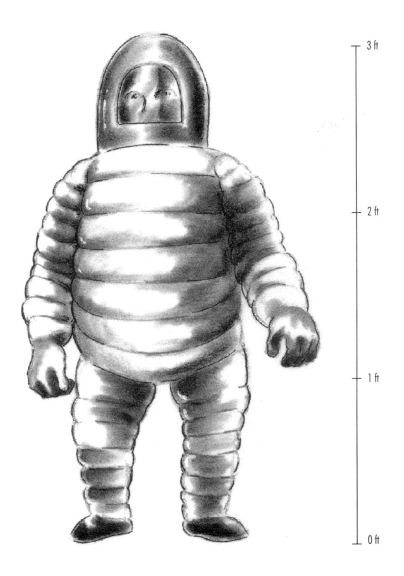

3 ft

2 ft

1 ft

0 ft

CLASS: *Humanoid*	DESCRIPTIVE INCIDENT
TYPE: *Short Non-Gray*	DATE: *February 24, 1977*
VARIANT: *4*	LOCATION: *Langenargen, Baden-*
DISTINGUISHING CHARACTERISTIC:	*Württemberg, Germany*
oval head and mouth	WITNESS: *Lothar Schaefler*

The central witness, a 25-year-old railway worker, was dropping a friend off at home at two in the morning after leaving a bar together, when they were blinded by the bluish white light of two approaching objects in the sky. The lights then stood still for five minutes, moved again toward one another, seemed almost to touch, and finally just "turned off" and disappeared.

When Schaefler's friend, an innkeeper, entered the house, he locked the door behind him. On his way up the stairs he saw that the unknown lights had reappeared, but as he approached a window, he felt paralyzed.

Meanwhile Schaefler felt terrorized by the object's enormous size and ran around the house looking for an open door. Seeking shelter, he then ran to the back door of a neighboring house. There he heard a short whistling sound, felt a draft of air, and suddenly saw two strange beings appear behind him.

They stood about four feet tall. Their bodies appeared human, though their hands reached their knees and their four fingers were webbed. Their skin was brighter than a human's. The only clothing he noticed was a frill like a harlequin's around their necks with six or seven light-green starlike serrations. Their heads were bare and perfectly round, as were their well-defined mouths. Schaefler did not notice or see a neck, ears, or nose on the entities. Their eyes, which were slanted like an Asian's but not as narrow, stared at him unflinchingly. As the beings approached, their torsos rocked back and forth.

After standing paralyzed for a while, Schaefler was able to move again, and he immediately panicked. He threw himself against the neighbor's locked door, smashed the middle pane, unlocked the door from the inside, and covered his face as he fell on the floor. When the tenants heard this, they called the police and found Schaefler lying there, his hand bleeding. The lights and the beings had disappeared. It was about 3:30 A.M., about an hour later than Schaefler thought it was.

The police took Schaefler to the hospital, where his blood alcohol was tested and found to be quite low. They concluded that the episode could not be explained as due to alcohol delirium. Schaefler suffered from insomnia in the weeks following the encounter, vomited several times at work, and developed a stomach ulcer.

Several other bar patrons reported seeing the object that night, and seven years later, the Italian Defense Ministry reported that an Italian fighter plane had been followed by a UFO for 23 minutes that night as well. Others explained the bright light seen that night as a meteor.

SOURCE: *Illobrand von Ludwiger, "The Most Significant UFO Sightings in Germany,"* MUFON 1993 International UFO Symposium Proceedings *(Seguin, Tex.: MUFON, 1993).*

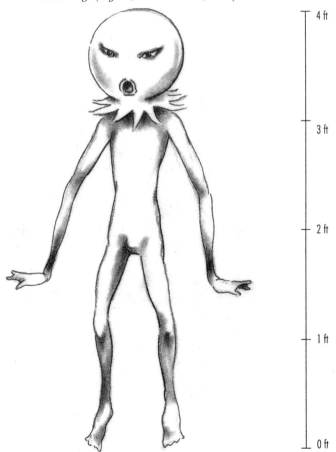

The witness, an enlisted soldier in the military police and an orderly assigned to Major Célio Ferreira, was fishing on a lagoon on a Sunday afternoon. Suddenly he heard voices, became aware of figures moving behind him, and felt a burst of light strike his leg. Da Silva dropped his fishing pole and fell to his knees.

Two beings, about four feet tall, wearing aluminumlike suits and what appeared to be helmets, seized him and dragged him to an object sitting on a dirt road. The object was shaped like an upright cylinder and had black platforms at each end. The soldier was taken inside, where the beings put one of their "helmets" on him. It was round in back, square in front with sharp edges, and flat from the forehead down but with a projection for the nose and round inch-wide holes for the eyes.

Da Silva felt the craft rise. The beings talked animatedly among themselves in a language he did not recognize. After a long period of travel, he felt a jarring that suggested their craft had landed. The soldier was then blindfolded and led to a large room, where they removed the wrap from his eyes.

A being stood in from of him who was extremely hairy and slightly taller than the rest. His waist-long hair was reddish and wavy. His wide-set eyebrows were two fingers thick and ran nearly straight across the forehead. His skin was light colored and pale. His deep-set eyes were greenish and round and slightly larger than a human's. His ears were also bigger, and so was his long and pointed nose. The being's mouth was wide and like a fish's. When the others took off their helmets, they were of similar appearance.

Da Silva watched as the beings, at one point more than a dozen, examined his fishing equipment and took one of every item he had in duplicate. Later the witness noticed on a low shelf the bodies of four human men, one black, and became terribly frightened. Later still, the beings gave him a dark green liquid to drink out of a cubical stone glass.

The dwarf leader then began a strange conversation with the

soldier, mostly about weapons, which was conducted entirely with gestures and drawings. Da Silva also understood that they wanted him to help in their relations with humans. When the soldier refused, the dwarf snatched the crucifix from the rosary Da Silva always carried with him. As the soldier began praying, a Christlike figure appeared to him, making revelations.

Shortly afterward, Da Silva was returned to Earth. As the machine landed, he lost consciousness and woke up near the town of Vitória, about 250 miles from where he had been fishing. He had a swollen knee and three open wounds on his shoulders where the helmet had rubbed against his skin. He had been away four and a half days.

SOURCE: *Hulvio Brant Aleixo, "Abduction at Bebedouro," in* Encounter Cases from Flying Saucer Review, *ed., Charles Bowen (New York: Signet, 1977), pp. 175–196.*

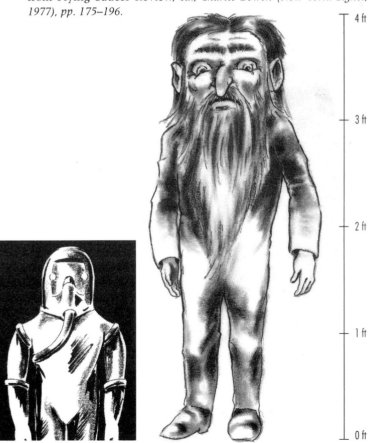

CLASS: *Humanoid*	DESCRIPTIVE INCIDENT
TYPE: *Short Non-Gray*	DATE: *July 25, 1979*
VARIANT: *6*	LOCATION: *Turis, Valencia, Spain*
DISTINGUISHING CHARACTERISTIC:	WITNESS: *Federico Ibáñez*
"eyes" and feet	

At 11:30 A.M., the witness, a 54-year-old farmer, was visiting some vineyards, which he owned, when he noticed something white and shining ahead. He thought it must be a neighbor's car. When he rounded the bend, the "motor car" was blocking the dirt road and Ibáñez pulled up behind it. But as he stopped, Ibáñez realized that the white object was not a car at all. It had no wheels and stood on two legs. The object resembled half an egg standing on its flat end. It was nearly nine feet high and almost three feet wide.

Suddenly the witness noticed two beings running toward the object. They stood about three feet tall and wore white shining outfits that reached down to their knees and covered their heads. At its widest, each outfit was about 16 inches. The beings had little black legs that ended in little feet that looked like "boxing gloves." Their faces were blank except for what appeared to be black protruding spectacles of some kind.

Within seconds the beings entered the object, which took off immediately, throwing up a cloud of dust. Ibáñez got back in his car, drove off to inspect his vines, and then returned to the site of his encounter. A subsequent investigation found four circular marks on the road forming a precise rectangle. The farmer, who knew nothing of UFOs, was held in high regard by the locals.

SOURCE: *Gordon Creighton, "The Encounter at Turis,"* Flying Saucer Review *27, no. 6 (June 1982): pp. 17–18.*

CLASS: *Humanoid*
TYPE: *Short Non-Gray*
VARIANT: 7
DISTINGUISHING CHARACTERISTIC:
hook nose and cone helmet

DESCRIPTIVE INCIDENT
DATE: *January 7, 1970*
LOCATION: *Imjärvi, Mikkeli, Finland*
WITNESSES: *Esko Viljo and Aarno Heinonen*

Viljo, a 38-year-old farmer, and Heinonen, a 36-year-old forester, had been skiing. At 4:45 in the afternoon they paused in a glade when they heard a buzzing sound and saw a bright light in the sky. Suddenly the light was enveloped in a reddish gray mist or cloud, the top of which emitted puffs of smoke.

As the cloud descended the witnesses noticed that inside was a round metallic object about nine feet in diameter. On its bottom were three hemispheres and a central tube. When the buzzing increased, the cloud disappeared, and the object descended to about 10 feet above the ground. A light beam then emerged from the central tube, illuminating a three-foot circle in the snow below. Heinonen felt as if someone was grabbing his waist and pulling him backward, so he stepped back a step and saw a creature appear in the light beam.

The creature was about three feet tall and had narrow slanting shoulders and thin arms and legs. It had a pale waxy face, small eyes, a curious hook nose, and small ears that narrowed toward the head. The creature wore light green overalls, darker green boots that stretched above the knees, and white gloves that reached above the elbows. Its clawlike fingers held a black box with a round opening that emitted a bright pulsing yellow light. On its head was a shiny conical helmet.

As the creature pointed the box's opening toward Heinonen, a thick reddish gray mist descended from the object. Large sparks, four inches long and colored red, green, and purple, emerged from the illuminated circle above the snow. The witnesses felt nothing when the sparks hit them. Soon the mist became so thick that the two witnesses could no longer see each other or the creature standing just nine feet away.

Finally the light beam seemed to retract back into the tube, the mist broke, and the air above them cleared. Heinonen felt that his right side had become numb, and when he tried to take a step forward on his skis, he fell. He abandoned his skis and with Viljo's help returned to the cottage belonging to Heinonen's parents. There he felt increasingly ill; he had a headache, difficulty breathing, body pains, vomiting, loss of memory, and urine as black as coffee. He continued to feel ill for months.

Viljo also had been physically affected. His face became swollen and red an hour after the encounter, and he later had difficultly with his balance, suffered a headache, and felt pain in his eyes. The doctor who examined both men believed that they had suffered a great shock. Their symptoms resembled those of radiation exposure. A reporter later located two independent witnesses who had seen a strange light in the sky late that day.

Heinonen went on to have many more UFO experiences in the years that followed and eventually became a "contactee."

SOURCE: *Sven-Olof Fredrickson, "A Humanoid Was Seen at Imjärvi,"* Flying Saucer Review *16, no. 5, (September-October 1970): pp. 14–18. Anders Liljegren, "The Continuing Story of the Imjärvi Skiers," parts 1 and 2,* Flying Saucer Review *26, no. 3, (September 1980): pp. 15–17; 26, no. 5, (January 1981): pp. 18–20.*

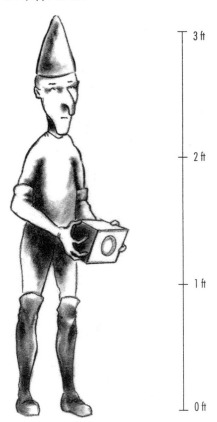

3 ft

2 ft

1 ft

0 ft

CLASS: *Humanoid*	DESCRIPTIVE INCIDENT
TYPE: *Short Non-Gray*	DATE: *August 19, 1970*
VARIANT: *8*	LOCATION: *Bukit Mertajam,*
DISTINGUISHING CHARACTERISTIC:	*Penang, Malaysia*
extremely small stature	WITNESSES: *Mohamad Zulkifli, Abdul Rahim, David Tan, Sulaiman, K. Wigneswaran, and Mohamed Ali*

Six schoolboys, aged eight to 11, at the Stowell English Primary School claim that a soup-plate-size flying saucer landed near them while they were busy playing cops-and-robbers near the school. When the tiny object landed, five "horrible-looking" three-inch-high spacemen put out a plank and emerged from the saucer. Four of the spacemen wore blue uniforms; one wore yellow. The one in yellow looked to the boys like "the leader," and sported "horns," stars on his shirt, and high boots.

The five beings were armed with miniature space guns. When the spacemen began installing what looked to be an aerial on a tree, Wigneswaran tried to capture the leader. At that point the leader fired his tiny space gun. The other boys then got scared and ran away. Wigneswaran was later found lying in the bushes by a school official. A small red dot appeared on the boy's right leg where he had been "shot."

Some of the other boys reported subsequent encounters with the tiny spacemen the following day. Though the headmaster, who felt the whole thing was a figment of their imagination, questioned the boys carefully, they all insisted on the truth of their story. Although this report is replete with classic science fiction elements, it is by no means the only report in the literature of beings of such extremely small stature.

SOURCE: *"Very Little Men!" (drawn from original newspaper reports), Flying Saucer Review 6, no. 6 (November-December 1970): pp. 29–30. Ahmand Jamaludin, "A Wave of Small Humanoids in Malaysia in 1970," Flying Saucer Review 28, no. 5 (June 1983): pp 24–27.*

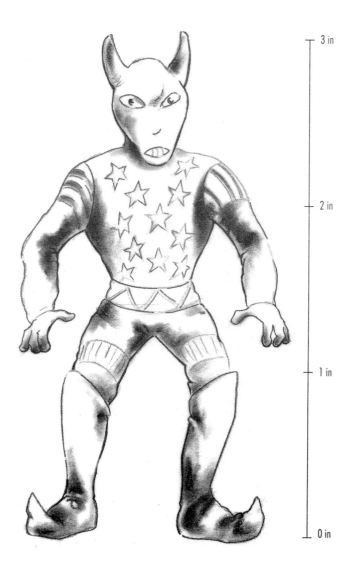

3 in

2 in

1 in

0 in

CLASS: *Humanoid*	DESCRIPTIVE INCIDENT
TYPE: *Giant*	DATE: *September 27, 1989*
VARIANT: *1*	LOCATION: *Voronezh, Russia*
DISTINGUISHING CHARACTERISTIC:	WITNESSES: *Vasya Surin, Genya*
three eyes	*Blinov, Julia Sholokhova, and*
	40 adults

At about six o'clock in the evening several schoolchildren and numerous adults saw a large spherical object hovering over a park. When a hatch opened in the bottom, a being appeared. It stood about 10 feet tall, had no neck, and wore silver overalls and bronze-colored boots. The being had three eyes; two were whitish, but the middle eye, or lamp, as one witness called it, was red and devoid of a pupil.

The being scanned the terrain, the hatch closed, and the sphere descended, brushing against a poplar tree, which bent and stayed in that position. The object, which measured about 45 feet wide and 19 feet high, then landed. The tall being emerged accompanied by a small robot, actually a box with something resembling a head on top of it. When the being uttered something, a small luminous triangle appeared on the ground, but at another utterance, it disappeared. The being then adjusted something on the robot's chest.

When a young boy began crying, the being, whose eyes seemed to emit light, looked at him. The boy froze. When the witnesses started shouting, the sphere and beings immediately vanished. But five minutes later the object and being reappeared. It now held a four-foot-long tube at its side. When the being pointed it at a nearby teenage boy, the boy disappeared. The being then reentered the sphere, and as the object flew away, the boy reappeared.

Some witnesses reported having seen a symbol, known as UMMO, on the being's belt and on the object. This design had been reported in several close encounters in Spain during the 1970s. Most investigators believe it was all a clever hoax by a small cult claiming contact with an extraterrestrial civilization. A report on UFO shapes, which had been published in Voronezh, had included the UMMO symbol, and investigators believed that this had contaminated an otherwise solid case.

SOURCE: *Jacques Vallee,* UFO Chronicles of the Soviet Union: A Cosmic Samizdat *(New York: Ballantine, 1992).*

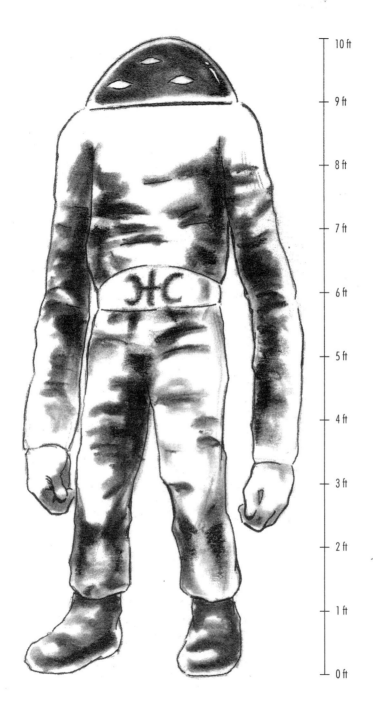

10 ft

9 ft

8 ft

7 ft

6 ft

5 ft

4 ft

3 ft

2 ft

1 ft

0 ft

CLASS: *Humanoid*	DESCRIPTIVE INCIDENT
TYPE: *Giant*	DATE: *August 28, 1963*
VARIANT: *2, aka "Cyclops"*	LOCATION: *Belo Horizonte, Minas*
DISTINGUISHING CHARACTERISTIC:	*Gerais, Brazil*
one eye	WITNESSES: *Fernando and Ronaldo*
	Eustáquio Gualberto and
	José Marcos Gomes Vidal

After dinner at about 7:30 P.M., the three boys went out into the garden to wash out a coffee percolator with water from a drum that stood by the well. The Moon was out and the garden was brightly illuminated. As José Marcos, the seven-year-old from across the street, lowered his head into the tank to scoop up water with a bowl, Ronaldo, seven, and his brother Fernando, 12, noticed that the bright light actually came from a spherical object about 10 feet wide that was hovering just over the pear tree in front of their house. The sphere was divided into squares and had three antennalike rods sticking out from the top.

Through its transparent walls, the boys could see four beings, all wearing what appeared to be divers' suits and clear helmets. They were seated on one-legged stools. One of the beings appeared to be female, judging from the long, pulled-back blond hair; the others, all bald, were apparently male.

Suddenly, one of the men, who seemed about 10 feet tall, floated down to the ground between two parallel shafts of yellow light shining from the underside of the sphere. Through his transparent helmet, which had a hoop-shaped antenna on top and a small round ball hanging from it, the boys could see that the being had only one large round all-dark eye. Above this frequently moving eye was a dark protuberant area that resembled an eyebrow. The being's face had a reddish tint. The rest of his body was covered with a leatherlike uniform that seemed wrinkled at the limbs and chest. It was brown up top, white below the waist, and black from the knees down. These were apparently boots.

With a measured step, the enormous being headed toward José Marcos, who had his head in the water drum. Seeing a threat, Fernando jumped on José Marcos and threw him on the ground in an effort to protect him. The being then looked at the boys, who now felt powerless to flee or shout, and began speaking strange words and gesturing with his hands and head.

When the being moved to sit down on the edge of the well, Fernando ran behind the entity, picked up a chipped brick, and raised it to throw at him. Suddenly the giant jumped up, and a beam of yellow light emerged from the rectangular area at the level of his chest and struck Fernando's hand, causing him to drop the brick. The being, who had a copper-colored box on his back, again began speaking in a loud voice, apparently trying to make himself understood.

Finally the being gave up and floated back into the sphere, which then brightened, rose silently, and vanished from sight. The boys then ran into the house and reported the encounter to their mother. José Marcos crawled under a bed. The father later found small triangular marks about three inches deep along the path where the boys said the mysterious being had walked.

SOURCE: *Gordon Creighton, "The 'One-Eyed Entities' of Belo Horizonte,"* Flying Saucer Review, *special issue no. 3 (September 1969): pp. 28–32.*

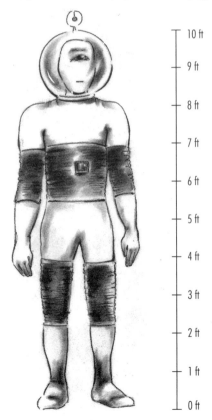

CLASS: *Humanoid*	DESCRIPTIVE INCIDENT
TYPE: *Giant*	DATE: *September 12, 1952*
VARIANT: *3*	LOCATION: *Flatwoods, West Virginia*
DISTINGUISHING CHARACTERISTIC:	WITNESSES: *Kathleen, Eddie, and Fred*
headpiece and claws	*May; Gene Lemon; Neil Nunley;*
	Ronnie Shaver; and Tommy Hyer

Shortly after sunset five youngsters observed what they thought was a "meteor" pass over them and land atop a nearby hill. (Similar reports of a strange light in the sky came from other central Atlantic states that night.) On the way up the hill, the boys stopped by the home of Kathleen May, mother of Eddie and Fred, and persuaded her and Gene Lemon, a 17-year-old National Guardsman, to join them.

Proceeding in the direction of the fallen object, the group came upon a surprising sight—about 75 feet away among the trees was a pulsating object or "ball of fire" about 20 feet in diameter and six feet high. One boy thought he saw some animal eyes in the trees. The dog with them began growling, and its hair stood on end.

When Lemon shone his flashlight through the mountain fog, the group saw a huge figure standing beneath the lower branches of a tree. It was 10 to 15 feet tall and had a bloodred face with two greenish orange eyes that glowed like a wild animal's. The head had a pointed hood shape around it, and the body was draped in a garment similar to a monk's. As the "monster" began floating toward them, it made a hissing sound.

The group, extremely frightened, fled down the hill. Kathleen May was hysterical, some of the youngsters were treated for shock, and some "vomited for hours" from the pungent irritating odor that had permeated the hill. About an hour later the local sheriff led a posse armed with shotguns and searched the hill but found nothing other than the sickening odor still lingering over the area. The following day the editor of the local paper found two parallel skid marks and a large circle of flattened grass where the pulsating object had been seen.

SOURCE: *Coral and Jim Lorenzen,* Flying Saucer Occupants *(New York: Signet, 1967).*

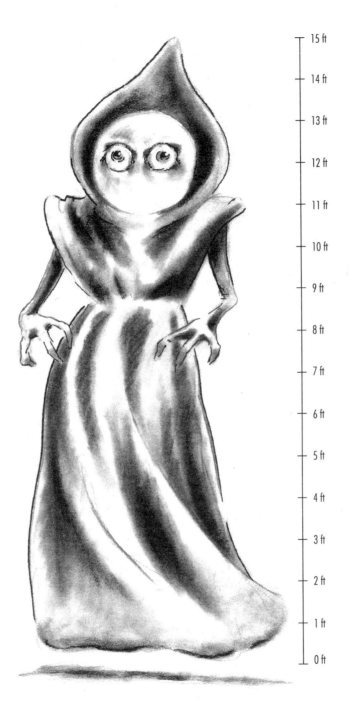

CLASS: *Humanoid*	DESCRIPTIVE INCIDENT
TYPE: *Giant*	DATE: *May 29, 1986*
VARIANT: *4*	LOCATION: *Santa Rosa, La Pampa,*
DISTINGUISHING CHARACTERISTIC:	*Argentina*
long hands	WITNESS: *Oscar Alberto Flores*

Dogs barking and a loud buzzing noise outside the house awoke the 28-year-old Flores, who on opening his bedroom window saw an object hovering above the treetops. Turning around, he noticed two beings standing at his bedroom door.

The beings were about eight feet tall and had long, thin hands, each of which had only three fingers, the middle one being the longest. Their faces were expressionless since they lacked a nose, mouth, or ears. Their eyes were small and dark. Flores could not see their legs, as they were obscured by the bed.

The beings wore tight-fitting silvery overalls, a belt from which hung accessories, and a necklace with a large medallion. The beings gesticulated constantly, but Flores understood nothing of their meaning.

Then, as suddenly as they had appeared, the beings vanished. Flores immediately went outside and saw a ball-shaped object heading south. He then left for the police station to report the incident. Flores claims that his face peeled after the contact. His parents and friends also noticed a change in his personality. Flores, the extrovert, had become a worrying introvert.

SOURCE: *Fabio Picasso, "Infrequent Types of South American Humanoids: Part 1,"* Strange Magazine, *no. 8 (fall 1991): pp. 21–23, 44.*

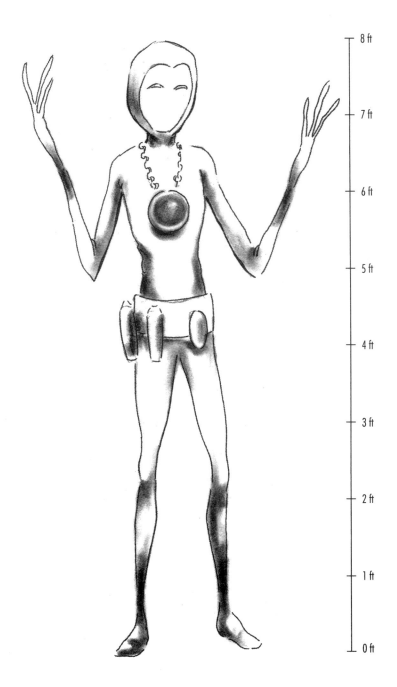

8 ft

7 ft

6 ft

5 ft

4 ft

3 ft

2 ft

1 ft

0 ft

CLASS: *Humanoid*
TYPE: *Nonclassic*
VARIANT: *1, aka "Mummy"*
DISTINGUISHING CHARACTERISTIC:
elephant skin and head "points"

DESCRIPTIVE INCIDENT
DATE: *October 11, 1973*
LOCATION: *Pascagoula, Mississippi*
WITNESSES: *Charles Hickson and
Calvin Parker*

The witnesses were fishing from an old pier in an abandoned shipyard on the Pascagoula River. Shortly after nightfall Hickson, looking around to bait his hook, saw a domed, football-shaped object descend until it hovered just off the ground about 30 feet away from them. The large craft had two windows and two blue lights, and made a buzzing sound. When the object landed, an unseen door opened to reveal a brilliantly lit interior. Three beings came out and floated toward the witnesses.

These beings were about five feet tall. Their skin was so gray and rough, like elephant skin, that they looked like mummies. No clothes were apparent. On their faces was something about two inches long that came out to a point and resembled a nose. They had a slit for a mouth, which never opened. If they had eyes, Hickson couldn't seen them, as the area above the nose was too wrinkled. They had no neck and their ears were pointed and retractable. Their arms were unusually long, and their hands were like mittens with a thumb attached. Their legs never moved but stayed together like a pedestal. Their feet were elephant-like.

When two of the beings grabbed Hickson by the arms, he felt a pain in his left shoulder. This immobilized him and allowed his captors to lift and float Hickson over and into the craft. The third being seized Parker, who immediately went limp.

Once inside, Hickson was nearly blinded by the light but was unable to close his eyes. He saw no furniture inside, only a screenlike device on the wall. He hung suspended in the air at a 45-degree angle while an eyelike device appeared out of the wall in front of his face and circled around him.

The beings who held Hickson during his examination moved in a stiff mechanical way but did their work with speed and efficiency. One made a buzzing sound. The beings then disappeared for some time. When they returned, they grasped Hickson again and floated him through the opening, which had reappeared, and took him back to the place where they had found him. His legs collapsed when he touched the ground. Parker stood by with a terrified look on his face.

Meanwhile the buzzing sound and blue light resumed, and the craft rose straight up and disappeared almost instantly. Hickson "heard" a message in his mind that the beings were peaceful. Though the two witnesses knew they would be ridiculed, they nevertheless told their story to the police.

SOURCE: *Charles Hickson and William Méndez,* UFO Contact at Pascagoula *(Tucson: Wendelle C. Stevens, 1988).*

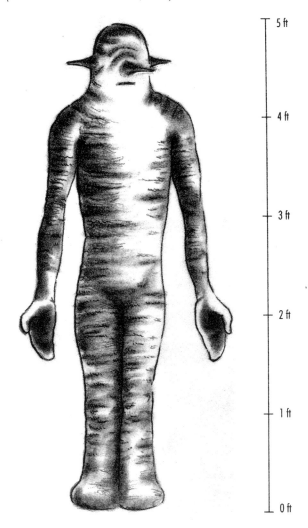

CLASS: *Humanoid*	**DESCRIPTIVE INCIDENT**
TYPE: *Nonclassic*	**DATE:** *August 8, 1993*
VARIANT: *2*	**LOCATION:** *Belgrave, Victoria,*
DISTINGUISHING CHARACTERISTIC:	*Austraila*
solid black coloring	**WITNESSES:** *Kelly Cahill and her*
	husband, and Bill, Jan, and Glenda

Sometime after midnight Kelly Cahill, a 27-year-old mother of three, and her husband were heading home after visiting a friend in the Dandenong foothills, when they saw a craft hovering silently above the road in front of them. The craft was round with windows around it and lights on the bottom. Just as Kelly told her husband that she thought she saw people in there, the craft shot off to the left and disappeared.

But a kilometer away they encountered a light so bright that Kelly had to hold a hand to her brow to see better. "What are you going to do?" she asked her husband, her adrenaline pumping. "I will keep driving," he said, and the next moment, Kelly, suddenly perfectly calm, said to her husband, "What happened? I swear I had a blackout." By the time they got home, Kelly realized she smelled of vomit and felt she had lost an hour of time. She found a triangular mark on her navel that night, and in the weeks that followed she entered the hospital twice, once for a uterine infection, the second time for severe stomach pains.

Later Kelly consciously remembered that when the road had curved ahead of them, the light that they had thought was in front of them on the road was actually on the right at the bottom of a gully in a field. The object was massive, about 150 feet wide. Kelly had asked her husband to stop the car. They had both gotten out, crossed the road, and seen another car stopped down the road. All of a sudden they saw an all-black figure in the field, about seven feet tall and not human. Its eyes were big like a huge fly's and glowed red.

Then she realized that there were "heaps of them" in the field. One group of beings approached them rapidly, as if gliding, while another group approached the people in the other car down the road. Kelly had a sense that the beings were evil, that they lacked souls. Struggling to stay conscious at that point, she heard her husband say "Let go of me," and suddenly she felt herself getting sick. Later, an angry and frightened Kelly screamed at the creatures. The next thing she remembered was being back in the car.

62

Kelly experienced a series of dreams about the encounter. In one she saw the being leaning over her as if he was about to kiss her navel. The creature was tall, had a larger-than-normal head, long thin arms, a bulging abdomen, and skin like gray-black plastic. "The creature was black," said Kelly, "but not the color black. It was as if someone had cut a hole in matter where he stood or as if he himself was a hole in space." The independent witnesses in the other car have confirmed Kelly's description of the object and the beings—except that they did not recall the creature's red eyes.

A similar all-black being with long arms was seen in Leicester, England, in the summer of 1928.

SOURCE: *Bill Chalker, "An Extraordinary Encounter in the Dandenong Foothills,"* International UFO Reporter *19, no. 5, (September-October 1994): pp. 4–8, 18–20.*

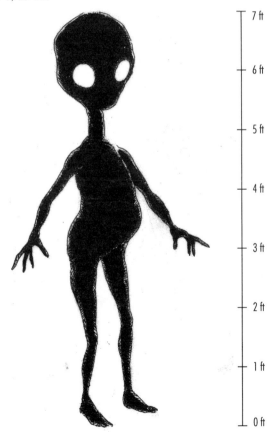

CLASS: *Humanoid*	**DESCRIPTIVE INCIDENT**
TYPE: *Nonclassic*	**DATE:** *October 25, 1974*
VARIANT: *3*	**LOCATION:** *Rawlins, Wyoming*
DISTINGUISHING CHARACTERISTIC:	**WITNESS:** *Carl Higdon*
lack of hands	

The witness, an oil driller in his early forties, was elk hunting on the northern boundary of the Medicine Bow National Forest when he spotted five elk and fired at the bull. But the bullet "went only about 50 feet and dropped" as if it had struck a wall. When Higdon heard a twig snap, he turned to see a humanlike figure in the shadow of a nearby tree.

The "man" was bowlegged, stood about six feet two and weighed about 180 pounds. He wore a black suit and black shoes. One belt crossed his breast; another his waist. The waist belt had a star at the buckle and a yellow emblem on an apronlike flap beneath it. His face was nearly human but was sloped and without a chin. The nose was flat, the brows were hairless, and the ears were not visible. His mouth showed but six teeth, three above and three below. The hair on his head was thin and stood up like straw. Higdon saw no hands on the "man," but his right arm ended in a cone-shaped device, which Higdon called a gun.

The "man" called himself Ausso and offered Higdon a packet of four pills. Ausso claimed they satisfied one's hunger for four days. Higdon took one, though ordinarily he never even took aspirin. Ausso then invited Higdon to come along and he accepted. When Ausso pointed his right arm, Higdon suddenly found himself inside a transparent cubicle, strapped to a chair and wearing a helmet. In the cubicle were four seats, a mirror, a control panel, another being like Ausso, and the five elk frozen still in a kind of cage behind him.

When Ausso pointed his arm at the controls, the cubicle began moving and Higdon saw Earth receding below him. Moments later they landed on a dark planet that Ausso said was 163,000 light years away. Outside the cubicle was a huge tower with a bright rotating light, making a sound like an electric razor. Standing in the nearby plaza were what looked like five humans in conversation—two blond teenage girls, one teenage boy, a slightly younger girl, and a gray-haired man of 40 or 50.

When Ausso pointed his arm again, Higdon found himself

inside a room in the tower. A shieldlike device came out of the wall in front of Higdon for several minutes, then retracted. At the end of this examination, Ausso told Higdon he was not what they needed and would be taken back. Ausso returned Higdon's rifle regretfully and floated the remaining pills out of his pocket.

Higdon then found himself standing on a rocky slope back on Earth, where he fell and injured himself. About two and a half hours had passed. He found his truck in a place where the terrain was too rough for him to drive into or out of. He called for help on his CB. The rescue party found Higdon disoriented and confused, and his truck had to be towed out. He began relating this episode while in the hospital.

A nearly identical armed being was observed by an eight-year-old boy in Wales in July of 1976.

SOURCE: *Coral and Jim Lorenzen,* Abducted! *(New York: Berkley, 1977).*

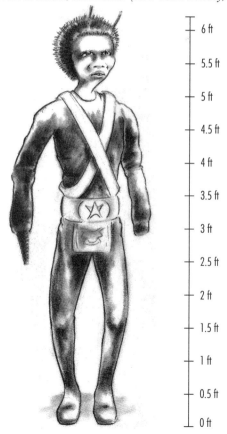

6 ft

5.5 ft

5 ft

4.5 ft

4 ft

3.5 ft

3 ft

2.5 ft

2 ft

1.5 ft

1 ft

0.5 ft

0 ft

CLASS: *Humanoid*	DESCRIPTIVE INCIDENT
TYPE: *Nonclassic*	DATE: *November 25, 1896*
VARIANT: *4*	LOCATION: *Lodi, California*
DISTINGUISHING CHARACTERISTIC:	WITNESSES: *Colonel H. G. Shaw*
soft downy fur	*and Camille Spooner*

Nearly a century before such claims became popular, Colonel Shaw and his friend were nearly abducted by what they took to be aliens and their craft. Shaw was putting together an exhibition for a fair in Fresno, and that day he and Spooner were traveling by horse and carriage toward Stockton. It was late in the afternoon when their horse became terrorized and froze. As the two men looked up, they saw three tall and thin figures with small delicate hands. They had no hair except for a soft downy fur on their skin. They had large eyes, but their mouths and ears were small. According to the witnesses, they seemed possessed of a "strange beauty."

Each being held a bag with a nozzle, which they put to their mouths as if to breathe. They also carried bright egg-shaped lamps. The beings seemed to communicate with one another in a kind of warbling "monotonous chant." The witnesses claimed that the beings had tried to abduct them but that Shaw and Spooner were apparently too heavy to be carried away by the lightweight creatures.

When the beings turned their lights on the nearby bridge, they illuminated a cigar-shaped craft hovering above the water. Swaying back and forth and almost drifting off the ground, the beings returned to their craft. They then sprung up into the air and floated down into a door on the side of the craft. The object then sailed away. Shaw was convinced that the beings had come from Mars.

SOURCE: *Jenny Randles,* Alien Contacts and Abductions *(New York: Sterling, 1994).*

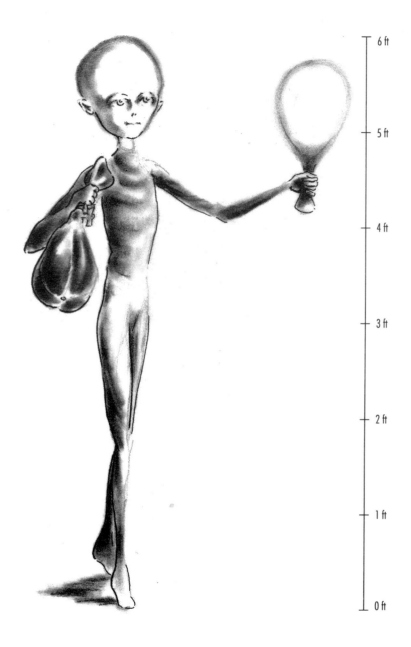

6 ft

5 ft

4 ft

3 ft

2 ft

1 ft

0 ft

ANIMALIAN

CLASS: *Animalian*	DESCRIPTIVE INCIDENT
TYPE: *Hairy Mammalian*	DATE: *October 25, 1973*
VARIANT: *1, aka "Bigfoot"*	LOCATION: *Greensburg, Pennsylvania*
DISTINGUISHING CHARACTERISTIC:	WITNESSES: *Stephen Pulaski and*
tall stature	*two 10-year-old children*

At about nine o'clock at night, a 22-year-old farmer and coal miner and some 15 others saw a bright red ball hovering high over a nearby field. The farmer decided to investigate, and a pair of fraternal twins hopped into the car with him. As they approached, the three witnesses saw the object descending. When they walked up over the crest of the hill, they came upon a dome-shaped object about 100 feet in diameter. The bright white object, which made a sound like a lawn mower, had either landed or was hovering just above the field.

Suddenly one of the twins spotted something walking along the fence. Pulaski, who wore glasses for myopia, raised his rifle and fired a tracer slug over the heads of the two figures. At first he thought they were bears, then realized that they were not.

The two creatures were taller than the six-foot fence. One was about eight feet tall, the other was a seven-footer. Both creatures were covered with long, dark, grayish hair, and their arms hung almost to the ground. Their eyes glowed a green-yellow color. The creatures made a whining sound, back and forth, as if in conversation with each other. And a strong odor, like burning rubber, was present.

When Pulaski realized that the creatures were headed toward them, one of the boys ran back home and Pulaski fired three rounds into the larger creature. Apparently hit, the creature made a whining sound and raised its hand toward the other creature. At that moment the bright object in the field just disappeared. The place where the object had been now glowed white. The creatures then slowly turned and walked back toward the woods.

Pulaski, whose eyes began to bother him, decided to report the incident to the police. When a trooper arrived at 9:45, he noted the glowing ring in the field and heard loud wailing noises in the woods. Suddenly Pulaski yelled that something was coming out of the woods toward them, and the two jumped into the patrol car and drove off.

Later still, at 2:00 A.M., when an investigating team arrived,

Pulaski, a six-foot-two, 250-pound man, went into a fugue, breathing heavily, growling, and flailing his arms. The group decided to leave the scene after Pulaski came out of his confused state, and the smell of sulfur or some other chemical began to permeate the area.

A psychiatrist who later examined Pulaski found no evidence of dishonesty, sociopathic behavior, or drug or alcohol use, either in connection with this incident or previously in his life.

SOURCE: *Berthold Schwartz*, UFO Dynamics *(Moore Haven, Fla: Rainbow Books, 1983)*.

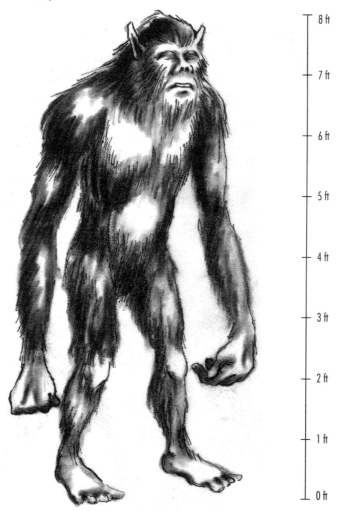

CLASS: *Animalian*
TYPE: *Hairy Mammalian*
VARIANT: *2*
DISTINGUISHING CHARACTERISTIC:
pointed ears

DESCRIPTIVE INCIDENT
DATE: *October 27, 1974*
LOCATION: *Aveley, Essex, England*
WITNESSES: *John and Sue Day and their children, Kevin, Karen, and Stuart*

After visiting relatives, the Days were on their way home, with two children sleeping in the backseat and the oldest, Kevin, listening to the radio. Their attention was drawn to a blue oval light that first paced their car and then passed in front of them. At about 10:10 P.M. and close to home, the Days lost sight of the object behind some high bushes on the right-hand side of the road.

But suddenly the Days felt that something was wrong. The sound of their car vanished and the radio crackled and smoked. Then, just before their headlights went out, they spotted a block of green mist on the road just ahead of them. The car jerked as it entered the mist, and after what seemed like a moment of silence and coldness, it emerged. A few minutes later they arrived home. But it was 1:00 A.M., nearly three hours later than it should have been.

Under hypnosis three years later, John Day revealed that while in the green mist, his family and their car had been teleported up a column of light into a craft, where they underwent medical examinations at the hands of a couple of four-foot-tall beings wearing loose white gowns. These neckless and slightly hunched over creatures had animal-like faces with large triangular eyes and large pointed ears. Short fur covered all their visible body parts, and their hands had four clawed digits. Occasionally the creatures made chirping sounds.

These beings seemed subservient to another set of beings aboard the ship, who stood about six and a half feet tall and wore suits that covered their hands and formed hoods over the heads. Though their mouths and ears were not visible, they looked nearly human, with the exception of their pink eyes. These taller beings seemed to run the show and escorted John and Sue on a tour of their three-level craft. During this tour the Days were given an explanation of the ship's propulsion system and shown a holographic movie of space that included the destruction of the aliens' home planet by pollution.

The car and family were then returned to a spot on the road

about half a mile from where they had been abducted. The family members reportedly underwent some major personality changes in the months following their encounter.

SOURCE: *Andrew Collins, "The Aveley Abduction,"* Flying Saucer Review *23, no. 6 (April 1978): pp. 13–25; 24, no. 1 (June 1978): pp. 5–15.*

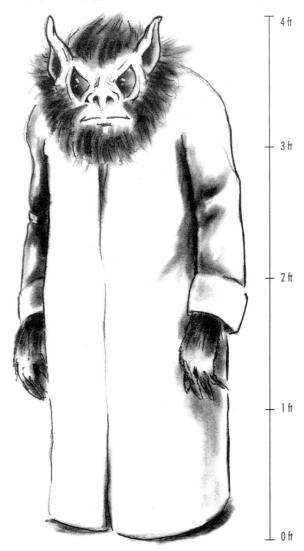

CLASS: *Animalian*	**DESCRIPTIVE INCIDENT**
TYPE: *Hairy Mammalian*	**DATE:** *November 28, 1954*
VARIANT: *3*	**LOCATION:** *Caracas, Venezuela*
DISTINGUISHING CHARACTERISTIC:	**WITNESSES:** *Gustavo Gonzales*
stiff bristly hair	*and José Ponce*

At two o'clock in the morning Gonzales and Ponce left Caracas in their flat panel truck to buy foodstuffs in Petare, 20 minutes away. Soon afterward they encountered a luminous sphere eight to 10 feet in diameter that nearly blocked the roadway. It hovered just six feet above the ground.

As Gonzales stopped the truck and the two got out to investigate, a little hairy man approached them. Gonzales immediately grabbed him, intending to take him to the police. To his surprise, Gonzales found the little man extremely light, weighing only about 35 pounds. His body was very hard and covered with stiff bristly hair. The little man gave Gonzales a push with one clawed hand and sent him flying about 15 feet. Ponce, who was Gonzales's helper, became frightened, and ran to the police station located a short distance away. As he departed he noticed two other little men emerging from the bushes. They were carrying either rocks or chunks of dirt in their arms as they hopped aboard an opening in the side of the sphere.

Meanwhile the first hairy little man, eyes aglow and claws extended, attacked Gonzales. Pulling out his knife, Gonzales stabbed the creature in the shoulder, but the knife glanced off as if the shoulder were made of steel. Then another little man emerged from the sphere and shot a beam of light from a small tube, momentarily blinding Gonzales. When the two little men climbed back aboard, the sphere took off rapidly.

Gonzales arrived at the police station shortly after Ponce. The two were suspected of being drunk, but an examination revealed otherwise. Gonzales was found to have a long red scratch on his side. The two were given sedatives. Several days later a doctor came forward, admitting that he had seen the fracas with the creatures but that he had left the scene, as he did not want to be involved in undesirable publicity.

SOURCE: *Coral E. Lorenzen,* Flying Saucers: The Startling Evidence of the Invasion from Outer Space *(New York: Signet, 1966).*

3 ft

2 ft

1 ft

0 ft

CLASS: *Animalian*
TYPE: *Hairy Mammalian*
VARIANT: *4*
DISTINGUISHING CHARACTERISTIC:
front feeler arms and tail

DESCRIPTIVE INCIDENT

DATE: *January 1958*
LOCATION: *Niagara Falls, New York*
WITNESS: *Anonymous*

This incident occurred one night during a violent snowstorm. It was 1:30 in the morning, and the witness, a woman who did not wish to be identified, was driving on the New York State Thruway. Since the visibility was very poor, she was driving very carefully, trying to locate the next freeway exit. She was on her way to visit her son, who was in the Army.

Suddenly she saw what she thought was a crashed airplane in the center parkway. But as she approached, she saw a large shape with a 50-foot-high illuminated rod that was slowly sinking into the ground. The car engine then died, the lights failed, and the car came to a stop. Stricken with panic, the woman tried to restart the engine, but to no avail.

At first she considered getting out of the car to see what was happening but thought better of it when she saw two shapes rising around the sinking rod. They were like animals with four legs and a tail, but they also had two feelers emerging from under their heads like arms. The creatures seemed to be suspended around and moving about the slim rod.

Suddenly the creatures disappeared, and the large shape rose up into the air. The witness could then see that it was saucer shaped. The craft spun up about 10 feet off the ground and then took off. At that point the woman's car lights came on, and she was able to restart the car.

Overwhelmed by curiosity, the witness then pulled up to where the object had been and got out to examine the spot with a flashlight. There she found a hole in the snow about a foot across, the grass showing underneath. She reported that it felt warm to the touch.

SOURCE: *Jacques Vallee,* Dimensions: A Casebook of Alien Contact *(Chicago: Contemporary Books, 1988).*

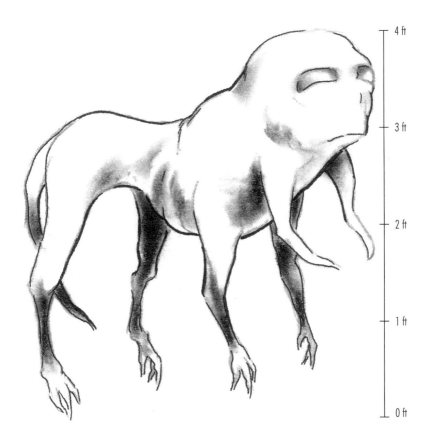

4 ft

3 ft

2 ft

1 ft

0 ft

CLASS: *Animalian*	DESCRIPTIVE INCIDENT
TYPE: *Hairy Mammalian*	DATE: *Early December 1974*
VARIANT: *5*	LOCATION: *Frederic, Wisconsin*
DISTINGUISHING CHARACTERISTIC:	WITNESS: *William Bosak*
calflike ears	

The night was unusually mild for early December, so there were patches of fog on the road when this 69-year-old dairy farmer drove home from a co-op meeting at 10:30 P.M. Bosak was driving slowly with low-beam headlights when he noticed something in the westbound lane. Slowing almost to a stop, Bosak saw a disk-shaped object that was partly obscured by fog and either close to or resting on the ground. The object was about six feet across and shaped like a chemistry lab bell jar. Bosak's headlights were the only source of illumination.

Inside the object's "curved front of glass" stood a strange figure with its arms over its head. Its eyes showed intense fright. The figure looked slender and was about six feet tall, covered with reddish brown fur. Its head was slightly rectangular, and its face was flat but hairless. The hair or fur, which ran over and along the side of its head, appeared swept back. The creature's eyes were humanlike, though they protruded slightly. Most peculiar, though, were the figure's calflike ears, which were long and stuck out some three inches.

As Bosak pulled up alongside and passed the object, his car lights dimmed, and the object took off, making a swishing sound. The witness, fearing ridicule, waited more than a month before telling his story to a newspaper reporter.

SOURCE: *Jerome Clark, "The Frightened Creature on County Road W,"* Flying Saucer Review *21, no.1 (June 1975): pp. 20–21.*

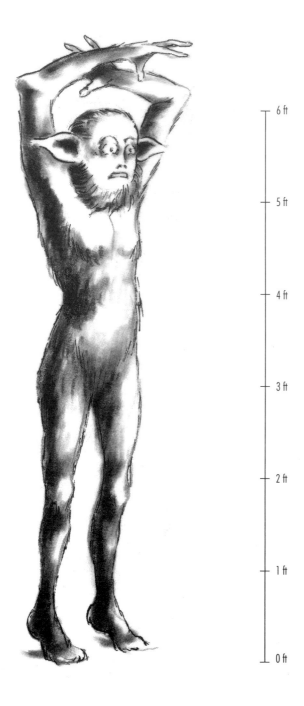

6 ft

5 ft

4 ft

3 ft

2 ft

1 ft

0 ft

CLASS: *Animalian*
TYPE: *Reptilian*
VARIANT: *1, aka "Swamp Creature"*
DISTINGUISHING CHARACTERISTIC:
"spines" on head

DESCRIPTIVE INCIDENT
DATE: *December 6, 1978*
LOCATION: *Marzano, Genoa, Italy*
WITNESS: *Fortunato Zanfretta*

As midnight approached, the 26-year-old night watchman decided to investigate four "torchlike" lights moving about horizontally three feet above the ground in the courtyard of an unoccupied summer house. When he tried to call the home office to report a possible case of housebreaking, Zanfretta's car lights and two-way radio failed. As he walked up to the gate, he held his flashlight in one hand and his gun in the other. The four lights began to move toward him, then disappeared behind the house.

When Zanfretta peered around the corner, he was suddenly pushed to the ground. As he turned to see his attacker, his head brushed up against the leg of a dark green 10-foot-tall being. Two huge luminous triangular yellow eyes, their outer corners inclined upward, were set in its head, which appeared to be two feet wide. At the sides of its head were pointed spines instead of hair and perhaps a pair of pointed ears or horns as well. On its forehead Zanfretta saw some luminous irregular wrinkles, which may have included a third eye. The being's body was a mass of dark gray horizontal folds of flesh or tubes.

The being then suddenly vanished, and Zanfretta fled back to his car. When a loud whistling noise broke out accompanied by a heat wave, he turned and saw a huge triangular craft rise up from behind the villa and shoot straight up into the sky. Zanfretta called for help on his radio, shouting, "They aren't men!" He noted that it was 12:16 A.M.—later than he thought it would be—and fainted next to his car. An hour later, colleagues found Zanfretta in a field far from his car. They later discovered a horseshoe-shaped impression about 24 feet wide.

Two weeks later, after complaining of persistent headaches, Zanfretta was placed under hypnosis. He described having been abducted into a hot, round room, where his monstrous kidnappers had placed something on his head that caused him great pain.

SOURCE: *Luciano Boccone, "Italian Night-Watchman Kidnapped by UFO,"*
Flying Saucer Review 26, no. 1 (Spring 1980): pp. 4–9.

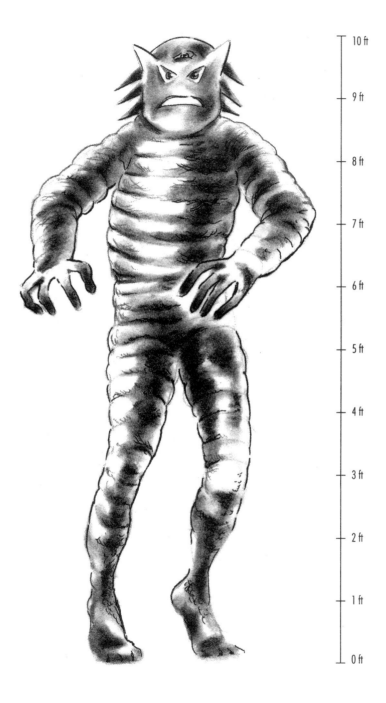

10 ft
9 ft
8 ft
7 ft
6 ft
5 ft
4 ft
3 ft
2 ft
1 ft
0 ft

CLASS: *Animalian*	**DESCRIPTIVE INCIDENT**
TYPE: *Reptilian*	**DATE:** *July 1983*
VARIANT: *2, aka "Lizard Man"*	**LOCATION:** *Mount Vernon, Missouri*
DISTINGUISHING CHARACTERISTIC:	**WITNESSES:** *Ron and Paula Watson*
webbed feet and hands	

It was morning on the Watson farm. Looking across the road, the Watsons noticed some bright silver flashes coming from the pasture across from their farmhouse. Through binoculars, which Ron and Paula passed back and forth, a strange scene came into focus. There were two silver-suited beings running their hands over a motionless black cow lying on the ground.

When the beings made jerky movements with their hands, the cow suddenly rose into the air and, with the beings, floated up into a cone-shaped object that stood near a clump of trees. Because the object's mirrorlike surface reflected its surroundings, it was nearly invisible.

Standing next to the object were two other strange-looking creatures. On the left side was a tall, green-skinned "lizard man." Its glaring eyes had the vertical pupils of a reptile. Its hands and feet were webbed. On the right side of the craft was a taller bigfoot-type creature that also had yellow vertical slits in round green eyes.

Though Ron wanted to get closer, Paula pleaded with him not to cross the road. Later, under hypnosis, Paula revealed that that she had been abducted by these beings just a few days before this incident.

When the beings entered the object with the cow, the object disappeared. Later the owner of the pasture told the Watsons that one of his black cows was missing. When the Watsons began to recount their experience, the farmer refused to listen. His black cow was never found.

SOURCE: *Linda Howe,* Glimpses of Other Realities, Volume 1: Facts and Eyewitnesses, *(Huntingdon Valley, Pa.: LMH Productions, 1993).*

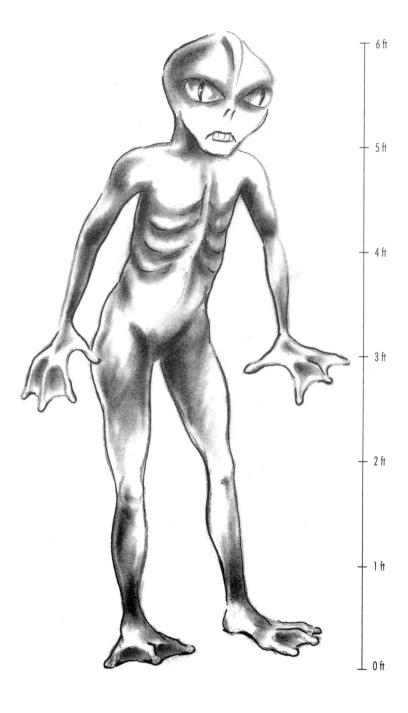

6 ft

5 ft

4 ft

3 ft

2 ft

1 ft

0 ft

CLASS: *Animalian*
TYPE: *Reptilian*
VARIANT: *3, aka "Goblin"*
DISTINGUISHING CHARACTERISTIC:
large hands with talons

DESCRIPTIVE INCIDENT
DATE: *August 21, 1955*
LOCATION: *Kelly, Kentucky*
WITNESSES: *Billy Ray Taylor, Lucky
Sutton, and the Sutton family*

At about 7:00 P.M. on a hot summer night, Billy Ray told the Suttons he had just seen a flying saucer with rainbow-colored exhaust fly across the sky and drop into a gully near their farmhouse. The Suttons laughed at his story. Half an hour later, the dog began barking and hid under the house.

When Billy Ray and Lucky went to the back door, they saw an approaching glow that turned out to be a three-and-a-half-foot tall creature with a round oversize bald head. The creature's skin was a silver metallic color and glowed in the dark. Its yellow eyes were large and set halfway around the side of its face. The creature's arms were almost twice as long as its legs and nearly touched the ground. Its hands were large and bore talons.

The men grabbed their guns, a .22 rifle and a shotgun, and waited until the creature was within 20 feet of the back door before opening fire. The shots sounded like they "hit a bucket," but the visitor simply flipped over backward and scurried off into the darkness. When another visitor appeared at the window, the men shot at it through the screen. Thinking the creature had been killed, Billy Ray went out the front door to find the body. As he paused momentarily under the roof's overhang, a clawlike hand reached down and touched his hair. The family screamed and pulled him back inside as Lucky ran out, turned, and fired at the creature, knocking it off the roof. Both men then fired at another creature in the maple tree nearby, but it, too, merely floated to the ground and scurried away.

Unnerved by the ineffectiveness of their guns, the family bolted themselves inside the house. But the creatures kept returning to peer in the windows, and after three hours the eight terrorized adults and three frightened children piled into two cars and headed off into town to the police.

The Hopkinsville police returned to the farmhouse with the family and surveyed the house and surroundings but found nothing. Shortly after the police left at 2:15 A.M., the creatures returned, staring into windows, curious but never hostile. Again the men responded with gunfire. This continued until a half hour before sunrise. That morning investigators returned but again found nothing.

Andrew Ledwith, an engineer with the local radio station, interviewed the family immediately. They gave him almost identical stories and exactly the same descriptions of the creatures. Though the family was soon inundated by the media, they never exploited their story, never tried to rationalize it, and never recanted it.

SOURCE: *J. Allen Hynek,* The UFO Experience *(Chicago: Henry Regnery, 1972); and Ronald Story, ed.,* The Encyclopedia of UFOs *(New York: Doubleday, 1980).*

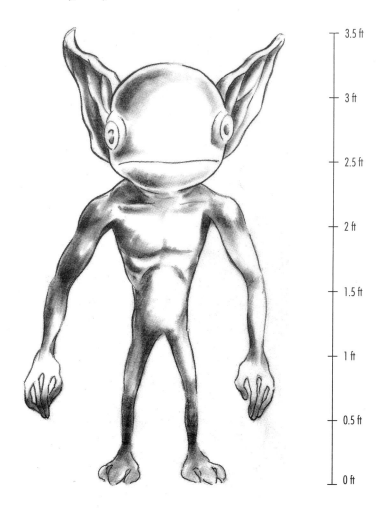

CLASS: *Animalian*
TYPE: *Amphibian*
VARIANT: *1*
DISTINGUISHING CHARACTERISTIC:
striped skin

DESCRIPTIVE INCIDENT
DATE: *September 24, 1951*
LOCATION: *Orland Park, Illinois*
WITNESS: *Harrison E. Bailey*

The 24-year-old steelworker was walking through the woods at 11:00 A.M. when he felt a cramping and burning sensation on his neck. When he turned around, he saw a gray object that he assumed was a "whirlwind." His next conscious memory was of seeing a silver gray oval like a water tank across the road on the edge of a meadow. Bailey, feeling paralyzed, then saw two strange men wearing what looked like green-tinted face shields at the craft's window. The men asked where he was from and where he was going. When the paralysis wore off, Bailey walked away, glancing back once at the strange ship. A short while later Bailey felt more cramping throughout his body and fatigue like he had never felt before. Suddenly it was late afternoon.

Though he had told no one of the incident, Bailey, a black man, was confronted the next day by a group of white men, who yelled at him. "Hey you," they said, "Did we see you come out of a flying saucer yesterday?" Shocked by the question, Bailey said "No."

Fourteen years passed before Bailey talked openly about this experience and his suspicion that it somehow was responsible for his chronic health problems. In 1966 he became a preacher, but he did not seek help for what he called his "flying saucer disease" until 1975, when under hypnosis details of that day a quarter of a century before emerged.

Bailey recalled having been swarmed in the woods by dozens of "froglike" creatures that walked. They were just a foot and a half tall and covered with smooth, brown, striped skin. They had little hands and only three toes on their feet. The creatures had slit mouths and prominent eyes that curled around the sides of their heads.

Suddenly the creatures clustered around him, jumping up to touch his hips and upper body. They seemed to talk to one another in high-pitched cries and sounded like wild ducks. All during this time the creatures were accompanied by numerous tiny "bugs," as Bailey called them, that scurried about in an erratic manner. They had dark round shells one inch in diameter.

Bailey was running to try to escape this alien horde when he came across the bus-size object just off the road. He remembered awakening inside the craft and speculated that the froglike creatures must have bit him or otherwise put him to sleep. Two beings, each five feet tall, then approached Bailey inside the ship. He avoided looking at them too closely but recalled seeing flattened and bizarre features beneath their tinted shields. Before being released, Bailey was given a message telepathically: They meant no harm and desired to land and communicate with humankind. They also wanted him to be a spokesman for them. Bailey would again be visited by these aliens in 1977 and 1978.

SOURCE: *Ann Druffel, "Harrison Bailey and the 'Flying Saucer Disease,'" in* UFO Abductions, *ed., D. Scott Rogo (New York: Signet, 1980), pp. 122–137.*

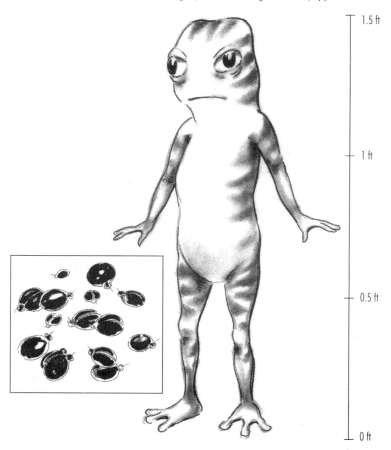

CLASS: *Animalian*	**DESCRIPTIVE INCIDENT**
TYPE: *Amphibian*	**DATE:** *January 25, 1967*
VARIANT: *2*	**LOCATION:** *South Ashburnham,*
DISTINGUISHING CHARACTERISTIC:	*Massachusetts*
eyes on stalks	**WITNESSES:** *Betty Andreasson*

It began at 6:35 P.M. with the house lights going out briefly. Betty was in the kitchen, while her seven children and her mother and father were in the living room. She noticed a pulsing orange light streaming in the kitchen window and went in to calm the children. She then returned to the window with her father, and they both saw five strange-looking creatures leaping like grasshoppers toward the house. As the beings passed through the wooden door, everyone in the family blacked out except Betty.

What transpired afterward emerged under hypnosis several years later. The alien leader, who was the tallest, spoke to Betty telepathically and identified himself as Quazga. All the beings were about four feet tall, wore blue coveralls, and had pear-shaped heads and wraparound catlike eyes. Their sleeves displayed an insignia of a bird.

When Betty expressed concern for her family, they released her 11-year-old daughter, Becky, from unawareness, and one of the beings began playing with her, juggling balls of light. Betty gave Quazga a Bible, and he handed her a blue book. Then Betty was taken aboard a large, saucer-shaped object with a central superstructure. The object rested on the hillside in her backyard.

The craft then took off and merged with a larger craft, where Betty was subjected to probing with a variety of instruments, including one she called a cleaning device. During the medical examination that followed, the beings stuck a needlelike device up her nostril and later in her navel to test for procreation.

Afterward Betty put her clothes back on and was led to an enclosed glasslike chair where she sat for a while immersed in a liquid. She was then given something sweet to drink and led by two beings in silvery luminous suits with black hoods into a dark tunnel seemingly chipped out of stone. Together they went through a mirrorlike door and came out into a place with a vibrating red atmosphere. The black track they were following went between two square buildings with windowlike openings.

Suddenly Betty was frightened by a different set of beings

that crawled over the buildings. They were climbing up and down and in and out of the windows like monkeys. She described them as lemurlike creatures with full bodies but skinny arms and legs. The creatures were headless, however, though they had eyes on stalks that emerged from the top of their bodies. The stalks moved independently of one another and followed Betty and her companions as they glided by.

Shortly afterward, they entered a green realm full of plant life and water. Later, after seeing a gigantic bird turn to ashes in a phoenixlike fashion, Betty was returned home at 10:44 P.M. She interpreted the experience—one of many, it later turned out—as being angelic in nature.

SOURCE: *Raymond E. Fowler,* The Andreasson Affair *(Englewood Cliffs, N.J.: Prentice Hall, 1979).*

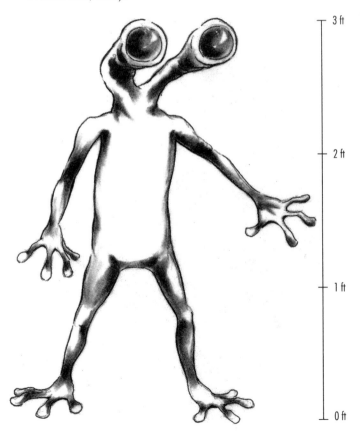

CLASS: *Animalian*	DESCRIPTIVE INCIDENT
TYPE: *Insectoid*	DATE: *A Friday evening in 1973*
VARIANT: *1, aka "Praying Mantis"*	*(or 1974)*
DISTINGUISHING CHARACTERISTIC:	LOCATION: *Cooksville, Maryland*
bowed legs	WITNESS: *Mike Shea*

One Friday evening after law classes at the University of Baltimore, the witness headed toward Olney to meet a friend at 7:00 P.M. About 15 miles outside of Baltimore, Shea looked to his left and saw a beam of light strike a barn 150 feet from his car. Hovering in the air was a huge object with a ring of alternating red and yellow lights. It was unlike anything the veteran had ever seen in Vietnam. His car window was open, and the object made no sound.

When the beam of light died out, Shea became fearful. He felt something coming up behind him. Suddenly he saw the object overhead and felt an electric current running down his spine. The next thing Shea knew he was approaching Olney and felt quite relaxed. When he arrived at the bar, his friend was nowhere in sight. The bartender told Shea that his friend had been there—at 7:00 P.M. Shea looked up at the clock. It was 9:00 P.M.

A decade later, the Washington lawyer decided to undergo hypnosis to resolve the lingering uneasiness and fear associated with that episode of missing time. During regressive hypnosis with abduction researcher Budd Hopkins, Shea remembered being too terrified to look at the object. As he continued driving, he saw four people at the side of the road. But they weren't people.

The creatures were dressed in black, in a kind of a plastic armor. Their faces were black. It looked as if they were wearing helmets with a line down the middle that came to a point. They actually looked like grasshoppers. They had long arms and bowed legs, like a monkey's. Three of the creatures were quite large. The fourth was small and was wearing a black silky suit with a zipper up the front. To Shea this being also seemed older—ancient, actually.

The witness remembered the mysterious light shining down from above as he stepped out of his car. The craft was nearby, and he could hear a low whir. Actually there were two craft: the smaller one on the ground and the larger one hovering above.

Later, inside one of the craft, Shea was put on a table and examined. Samples of various kinds were collected from his body.

SOURCE: *Gary Smith, "Unspeakable Secret,"* Washington Post Magazine
(3 January 1988): pp. 12–19.

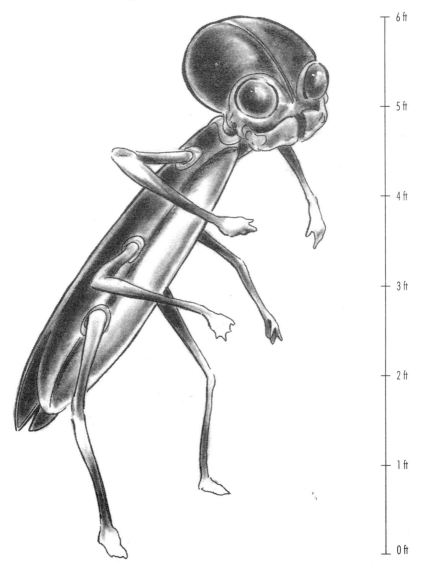

CLASS: *Animalian*
TYPE: *Insectoid*
VARIANT: *2, aka "Fairy"*
DISTINGUISHING CHARACTERISTIC:
rounded wings

DESCRIPTIVE INCIDENT
DATE: *January 4, 1979*
LOCATION: *Rowley Regis, West Midlands, England*
WITNESS: *Jean Hingley*

Early on a bitterly cold morning in a small town just west of Birmingham, the witness stood at her garden door waving good-bye to her husband as he left for work. On her way back inside she noticed a large orange sphere hovering close to the roof of the garage. Heat emanated from the object.

Suddenly her dog became stiff and flopped over sideways. At that moment three small figures slipped through the doorway into the house making a *zee, zee, zee* sound. Hingley headed toward the living room when she heard the Christmas tree rattling, only to find two of the beings shaking it.

The beings were three and a half feet tall and had large oval wings that looked as if they were made of thin paper and were covered with glittering "braille dots." Sparkling eyes like "black diamonds" were set wide on their white faces, which otherwise bore but the slightest hint of a nose and just a line for a mouth. Their heads were covered by helmets like goldfish bowls atop of which were set small lights. The beings had no apparent hands or feet, their appendages ending in simple tapered points. They were dressed in silver tunics with six silver buttons down the front and numerous thin streamers hanging down from the shoulders. The beings flew about and hovered with arms clasped over their chests and their legs hanging down stiffly.

Hingley felt paralyzed at times during the hour-long encounter. When she was able to speak to them, they replied in unison in a gruff masculine voice. The beings pressed the buttons on their tunics before they spoke. When she asked where they were from, they flew around the room and landed on the sofa, where they began jumping up and down like children.

When she told them to stop, the lights at the top of their helmets focused a very thin laserlike beam on her forehead that burned and occasionally blinded her. They disabled Hingley with the beam several times over the course of the encounter, seemingly whenever they were unable to perform tasks like drinking the water or eating the mince pies she offered them or answering questions. At one point the beings floated around the room, picking up and putting down cassette tapes and other things. It was as if the pointed ends of their arms were magnetic.

Finally the beings sailed out the back door, which had remained open the whole time, and into their spaceship, which measured eight feet long and four feet high. It had glowing port-holes around it and a scorpionlike tail at the back with an aerial wheel on top. The object took off and headed north.

Immediately afterward Hingley fell to the carpet in pain and only later was able to call her husband, her neighbors, and the police. An examination of the landing spot in the snow-covered garden revealed two parallel lines, each an inch wide, traversed by a series of lines like a caterpillar track. Her clock, TV, and radio ceased to work properly, and the cassette tapes the beings had handled were distorted and ruined. Hingley had sore eyes for a week after the encounter and a red mark on her forehead that persisted for months.

SOURCE: *Alfred Budden, "The Mince-Pie Martians: The Rowley Regis Case,"* Fortean Times, *no. 50 (summer 1988): pp. 40–44.*

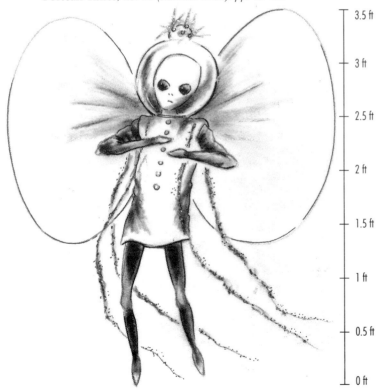

3.5 ft

3 ft

2.5 ft

2 ft

1.5 ft

1 ft

0.5 ft

0 ft

CLASS: *Animalian*	DESCRIPTIVE INCIDENT
TYPE: *Avian*	DATE: *November 16, 1963*
VARIANT: *1, aka "Mothman"*	LOCATION: *Hythe, Kent, England*
DISTINGUISHING CHARACTERISTIC:	WITNESSES: *John Flaxton, Mervyn*
headless	*Hutchinson, and two others*

Four young people in their late teens were walking along a country road at night when Flaxton, a 17-year-old painter and decorator, spotted a particularly bright "star" coming down out of the sky. The group became alarmed when the reddish yellow light seemed headed for them. It stopped to hover momentarily and then disappeared behind some nearby trees.

As the frightened youngsters took to their heels, they realized that an oval-shaped golden light was floating along beside them about 250 feet away and just 10 feet above the ground. The object was about 15 to 20 feet across and had a solid core. They noticed that when they stopped the light stopped, giving the four the impression that they were being watched.

The glowing object again disappeared behind the trees, and moments later there emerged from those trees a dark figure, stumbling toward them across the field. They described it as black, human size, but headless and possessing batlike wings on either side of its body. In addition, Hutchinson noted that the creature seemed to have webbed feet. The four took to their heels again and did not look back.

A week later investigators examining the site found a vast expanse of flattened ferns and three giant "footprints" measuring an inch deep, two feet long, and nine inches across.

Three years later a similar creature, which newsmen dubbed "Mothman," was reportedly seen over the Ohio River Valley in concert with strange lights in the sky.

SOURCE: *Charles Bowen, "Few and Far Between," in* The Humanoids, *ed., Charles Bowen, (London: Futura, 1974): pp. 19–20.*

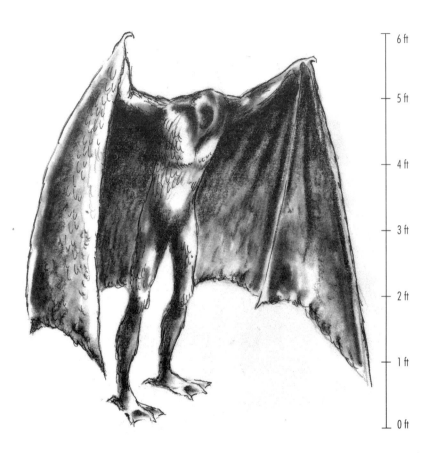

ROBOTIC

CLASS: *Robotic*	DESCRIPTIVE INCIDENT
TYPE: *Metallic*	DATE: *November 9, 1979*
VARIANT: *1, aka "Mines"*	LOCATION: *Livingston, Lothian,*
DISTINGUISHING CHARACTERISTIC:	*Scotland*
spikes	WITNESS: *Bob Taylor*

The 61-year-old forestry foreman had just parked his pickup truck in the woods and set off on foot with his dog to check out some trees in a clearing near a new highway. When he reached the clearing at about 10:30 A.M., he saw hovering just above the ground a gray sphere with several dark portholes above its ring-like rim. When Taylor tired to focus on the details, the object appeared to fade in and out of focus, as if trying to camouflage itself, the witness noted.

Suddenly two beachball-size things came rolling from the craft toward Taylor at a good clip, making a kind of suction noise. The "things," said Taylor, looked like "sea mines" with six "legs." Within moments, the "mines" were at his feet. Taylor smelled an odor so pungent that it struck him down unconscious.

About 20 minutes later Taylor recovered, hearing his dog bark. The witness was lying on the wet ground with a burning sensation on his chin and an itchy left thigh. The "things" and the object were gone. Taylor felt weak and nauseous and his throat burned. He struggled to get back to his truck and tried but failed to radio for help. He then attempted to drive but, lacking coordination, quickly got his truck stuck in the mud. He finally staggered home to his wife, who found him exhausted and dirty, his pants torn.

While a doctor examined Taylor, the police treated the case as a physical assault and began an extensive criminal investigation. At the site they found lines on the ground, indentations consistent with the imprint from a heavy object, and holes dug by the spiked balls as they "attacked" Taylor.

One skeptic suggested that Taylor had encountered ball lightning. But those who know the witness have testified to his sincerity and reject the notion of a natural explanation.

SOURCE: *Peter Jordan, "UFO Assault in Scotland," Fate (June 1983): pp. 68–74.*

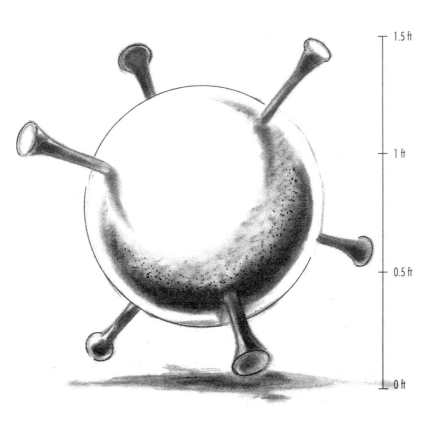

CLASS: *Robotic*
TYPE: *Metallic*
VARIANT: *2, aka "Tin Cans"*
DISTINGUISHING CHARACTERISTIC:
fins

DESCRIPTIVE INCIDENT
DATE: *October 23, 1965*
LOCATION: *Long Prairie,*
Minnesota
WITNESS: *Jerry Townsend*

At about 7:40 P.M., the witness, a rookie radio announcer, was about four miles out of Long Prairie when he rounded a curve into the twilight zone. Suddenly his engine, radio, and lights went dead. As he braked to a stop, he saw just ahead of him in the middle of the road a rocket-shaped object resting on three fins. The rocket stood about 30 to 40 feet high and measured about 10 feet wide.

Townsend got out of the car and saw three little beer-can-shaped robots coming toward him from under the rocket. Each robot was only about six inches tall and waddled side to side on a pair of fins. When they stopped, a third fin, like a stabilizer, came down in the rear. Though the robots had no faces as such, Townsend got the impression that they were watching him.

After what seemed to Townsend like an "eternity," the tiny robots returned to the craft and disappeared into it. When the rocket took off, it looked to him like someone was lifting a flashlight off a table. Townsend drove straight to the sheriff's office and recounted his experience.

The sheriff found Townsend visibly frightened and reported that the witness was not a drinker and that he enjoyed a good reputation in town. A police investigation of the site uncovered three parallel strips of an oil-like substance on the road about four inches apart and three feet long, the likes of which the police had never seen before on a road. Two hunters also came forward and seemed to at least partially corroborate Townsend's account, attesting that they had seen a bright object rise up from the area at the time of the incident.

SOURCE: *Coral Lorenzen, "UFO Occupants in the United States," in* The Humanoids, *ed., Charles Bowen, (London: Futura, 1974), pp. 168–169.*

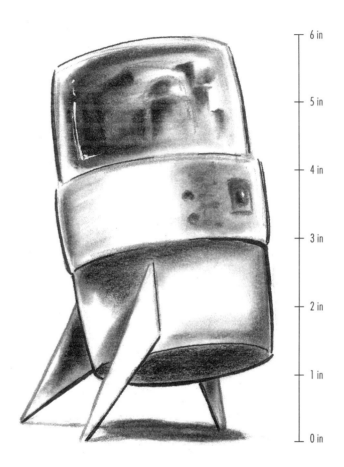

CLASS: *Robotic*
TYPE: *Metallic*
VARIANT: *3, aka "Slabs"*
DISTINGUISHING CHARACTERISTIC:
one-jointed arm

DESCRIPTIVE INCIDENT
DATE: *January 27, 1977*
LOCATION: *Prospect, Kentucky*
WITNESS: *Lee Parrish*

While driving home in a jeep at 1:05 in the morning, the 19-year-old witness observed a rectangular, fire-colored UFO just over the treetops. The craft measured about 10 feet high and 40 feet wide. Suddenly the jeep seemed to be under someone else's control and the radio failed. Parrish remembers being under the silent UFO at one point and seeing the craft speed away. He got home about 35 minutes later than the seven-minute drive home should have taken. His eyes hurt and his mother noted that they were bloodshot.

Under hypnosis Parrish recalled the source of that eye pain: It came from looking at the UFO. Once under it, his jeep had been suspended in midair while Parrish was transferred, without ever opening the jeep's door, into a large circular room.

Three machinelike beings stood in the room. The tallest one, a towering 20 feet high, was black and shaped like a tombstone with a small, featureless "head." Its "skin" was rough in spots, smooth in others. It also had a handless one-jointed "arm."

The smallest "being" stood less than six feet tall and was red and rectangular like a Coke machine. It, too, had one handless "arm," though it was not jointed. Parrish sensed the being was scared, though it slowly approached him and touched his head and shoulders, causing a cold stinging sensation. He later interpreted this as a physical checkup.

The third machinelike entity was white, about six feet tall, and bulkier than the others. It had a triangular "head" and two "arms," which it did not use. This glowing white being made the only sound—like someone brushing their teeth. Parrish got the impression that this one was the leader.

The three beings then seemed to merge into one another. First the smallest one went behind or merged with the white creature, and then the white one went behind or merged with the tall black entity. As the black entity began to back away, Parrish felt warmer. Suddenly the black being disappeared, and Parrish found himself back in the jeep, feeling that the beings would one day contact him again. The investigators were convinced of the witness's sincerity.

Similar "rectangular crewmembers" had been reported before; some had been seen during an early morning UFO encounter in Brazil in September of 1968.

SOURCE: *Carla L. Rueckert, "Kentucky Close Encounter,"* Flying Saucer Review *23, no. 3 (October 1977): pp. 15–16, 19.*

CLASS: *Robotic*	DESCRIPTIVE INCIDENT
TYPE: *Fleshy*	DATE: *September 10, 1954*
VARIANT: *1*	LOCATION: *Quarouble, Nord,*
DISTINGUISHING CHARACTERISTIC:	*France*
humanlike legs	WITNESS: *Marius Dewilde*

At about 10:30 P.M., the witness, a metalworker, stepped outside his house, located in a small town on the Belgian border, and saw a dark mass sitting on the railroad tracks. When he heard footsteps, Dewilde turned on the house lights and was confronted by two small beings, less than four feet tall, wearing very large helmets and heavy diving suits. He did not see any arms on them. An artist's rendering at the time shows they somewhat resembled George Lucas's *Star Wars* character R2D2.

As Dewilde moved toward the robotic creatures, a green ray shot out from the craft and paralyzed him. The pancake-shaped craft on the tracks looked to be about 10 feet high and about 20 feet long. By the time Dewilde regained his mobility, however, the entities were gone and the craft had begun to rise from the railroad tracks.

Four days later three investigators from the French air force interrogated Dewilde and thoroughly examined the site of the encounter. They discovered no trace of the entities, not even footsteps, which was not really surprising since the ground was hard. But they did find marks on the wooden railroad ties indicating that a heavy object had rested on them. In all, there were five marks on the tracks, all fresh and cut sharp. After consulting railroad engineers, they calculated that the ties had been subjected to a weight of 30 tons. The marks, the investigators assumed, had been left by the object's landing gear.

Something strange had taken place that night. Where the five marks had been found on the railroad ties, the roadbed gravel was notably brittle, as if calcined at high temperature. Further confirmation came from several inhabitants of the region who had seen a reddish light travel across the sky at about the time of the incident. This is one of the most famous events from the French UFO wave of 1954.

SOURCE: *Jacques Vallee,* Anatomy of a Phenomenon (*New York: Ace Books, 1965*).

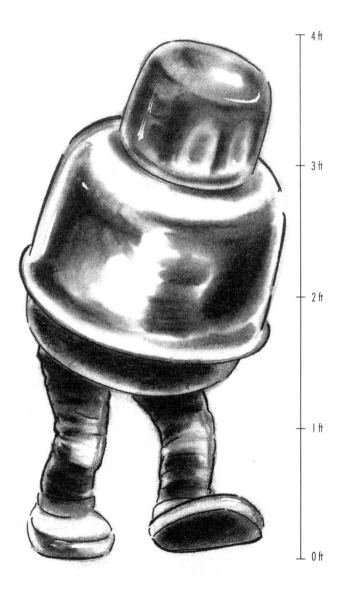

4 ft

3 ft

2 ft

1 ft

0 ft

CLASS: *Robotic*
TYPE: *Fleshy*
VARIANT: *2*
DISTINGUISHING CHARACTERISTIC:
square head

DESCRIPTIVE INCIDENT
DATE: *December 16, 1957*
LOCATION: *Old Saybrook, Connecticut*
WITNESS: *Mary Starr*

The former teacher was awakened sometime between two and three in the morning by a bright light in her bedroom. When she looked out the window, she saw a gray cigar-shaped object about 20 to 30 feet long hovering above her clothesline. The object was no more than 10 feet from her house.

Through the lighted portholes Starr saw two figures passing each other inside, their right arms raised, walking in opposite directions. Given the height of the craft, she estimates that the figures could not be more than three and a half to four feet tall. Their heads were square or rectangular and colored red orange with a bright red "bulb" in the center. Starr speculated that these might be helmets. The entities wore what looked like jackets that flared out at the base. She saw no hands at the end of their raised right arms. If the entities had "legs," she could not see them, as the lower portion of their bodies was not visible.

As a third being appeared, the portholes began to fade and the entire object began glowing brightly. From the top of the craft an antenna emerged that oscillated and sparkled, then retracted when the object got underway. After a few maneuvers, the object, which had small lights outlining its rim, tilted up and shot into the sky at great speed.

SOURCE: *Richard Hall, Ted Bloecher, and Isabel Davis,* UFOs: A New Look *(Washington, D.C.: NICAP, 1969).*

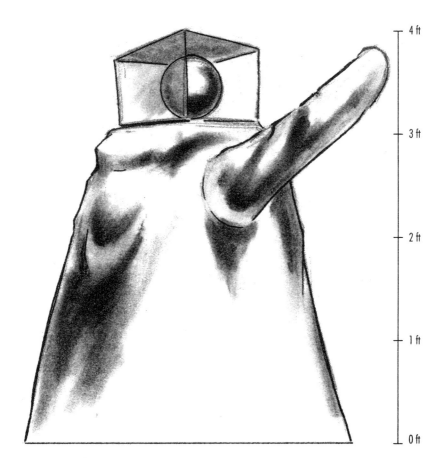

CLASS: *Robotic*
TYPE: *Fleshy*
VARIANT: *3*
DISTINGUISHING CHARACTERISTIC:
pedestal

DESCRIPTIVE INCIDENT
DATE: *September 15, 1977*
LOCATION: *Paciencia,*
Rio de Janeiro, Brazil
WITNESS: *Antonio La Rubia*

The witness, a 33-year-old bus driver, spotted a hat-shaped object more than 200 feet in diameter over a football field on his way to work at 2:20 in the morning. Frightened and ready to run, La Rubia was hit by a blue light, which immobilized him. At that moment three robotlike figures appeared near him.

The entities were about four feet tall and had an antenna more than a foot long jutting out from the middle of their football-shaped heads. The antennas were topped with a tea-spoon-shaped tip that rotated rapidly. Across the middle of their heads was a row of what looked like small mirrors in two shades of blue, one light, the other dark.

Their stocky bodies were covered in scalelike clothes or skin that appeared to be made of dull aluminum. They had arms like elephant trunks that narrowed down to tips as narrow as a finger. Across their "waist" was a belt with hooks holding syringe-like devices. From the bottom of their rounded bodies, emerged a single "leg," actually a narrow pedestal that ended in a small circular platform.

As the three identical entities floated around La Rubia, one pointed a "syringe" at him, whereupon he found himself in a corridor inside the craft. Through the transparent wall La Rubia could tell that they had taken off.

In a huge hall with only a pianolike device and filled with some two dozen of these entities, La Rubia underwent an examination of some sort. He was also shown a series of "slides," some of himself both dressed and naked, another of a horse and cart on a dirt road, one of traffic on a busy thoroughfare, and one of a dog trying to attack one of the beings. To La Rubia's horror the dog turned blue and melted. Another slide showed a "UFO Factory" with millions of robots around. During the "picture show," one of the entities drew blood from La Rubia's finger into a syringe.

Suddenly La Rubia thought he had been "thrown overboard," as he found himself on a street opposite the Paciencia bus station. One of the robots was standing beside him. When La

Rubia looked around, the being vanished and La Rubia looked up to see a huge, lead-colored balloon receding in the sky above him. It was 2:55 in the morning. Over the next month, the witness suffered from nausea, diarrhea, fever, and a burning and itching so severe that he was unable to work.

SOURCE: *Coral E. Lorenzen, "UFO Abduction in Brazil," in* UFO Abductions, *ed., D. Scott Rogo (New York: Signet, 1980), pp. 44–50.*

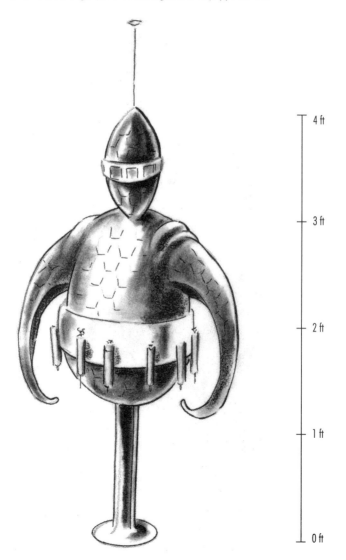

4 ft

3 ft

2 ft

1 ft

0 ft

CLASS: *Robotic*
TYPE: *Fleshy*
VARIANT: *4*
DISTINGUISHING CHARACTERISTIC:
shiny skin

DESCRIPTIVE INCIDENT
DATE: *July 1951*
LOCATION: *United States*
WITNESS: *Fred Reagan*

The witness claims he was flying a Piper Cub when his light aircraft was struck by a pulsating lozenge-shaped UFO. As Reagan, who had no parachute, and his wrecked aircraft were falling through the air, he began to feel like he was being drawn upward by what he described as a "sticky, clinging force." The next thing he knew he was drawn into the UFO.

Inside, Reagan found himself in the presence of small glistening beings. He described them as about three feet tall and looking like "huge stalks of metallic asparagus." The beings somehow spoke to him in English and apologized for the accident. They then gave him a medical examination, found that he had cancer, and removed it in exchange for the trouble they had caused him. The beings subsequently deposited Reagan, unconscious but without a single bruise, in a farmer's field near the wreckage of his aircraft. It should be noted that, after falling several thousand feet, the engine had embedded itself six feet into the ground.

Less than a year later, in May of 1952, Reagan died at the Georgia State Asylum for the Insane. The cause of death, according to a news report was "degeneration of the brain tissue due to extreme atomic radiation."

Reagan's bizarre story sat unpublished in the files of the editor of the English journal *Flying Saucer Review* for more than a decade. But while Reagan's account had seemed too preposterous and fantastic in the 1950s, by the late 1960s it had acquired a rather prophetic ring, as it possessed many features that had become rather commonplace in such accounts.

SOURCE: *Gordon Creighton, "Healing from UFOs,"* Flying Saucer Review 15, no. 5 *(September-October 1969): pp. 20–21.*

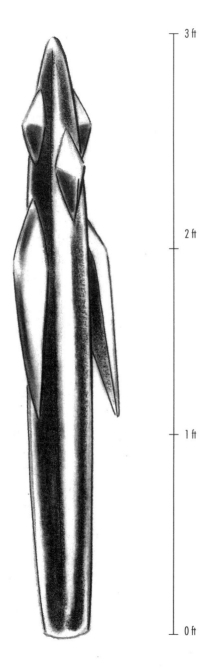

3 ft

2 ft

1 ft

0 ft

EXOTIC

CLASS: *Exotic*	**DESCRIPTIVE INCIDENT**
TYPE: *Physical*	**DATE:** *August 17 (or 31), 1971*
VARIANT: *1*	**LOCATION:** *Palos Verdes Estates,*
DISTINGUISHING CHARACTERISTIC:	*California*
"red spot"	**WITNESSES:** *"John Hodges" and*
	"Pete Rodríguez"

At two in the morning, the witnesses, young men in their twenties, were walking toward their car as a diffuse beam of white light shone from behind a clump of trees on a lonely road, three miles from the coast. When they got in their car and turned on the headlights, they consciously remembered being confronted by "extraterrestrial" beings about six feet ahead of them.

Hodges saw two; Rodríguez remembers only one. Both witnesses described the beings as resembling disembodied brains. Hodges said the larger one was about the size of the trunk of a human being and had a red spot, like a hematoma, on it, while the other, smaller being was the size of a softball. After staring at the strange things for a few seconds, the two frightened men drove off. When Hodges got home it was 4:30 A.M., two hours later than it should have been.

Five years later further details of the incident emerged under hypnosis. Hodges remembered seeing a mist around the two bluish brainlike beings. When the larger one came toward the car, Hodges recalled hearing a voice, telepathic he assumes, telling them to be careful, to better understand themselves, that they would be instruments of their own fate. As the being floated right outside the windshield, Hodges observed that the bright red spot, which he thinks may have been a growth, covered about one-eighth of the "brain."

After dropping Rodríguez off at home, Hodges remembered being in his car and having "a dream." He suddenly found himself back at the scene of the incident "talking" to the larger being. "Why do you come to me?" he asked, at which point he was enveloped by something and appeared in a large room where other, different beings were present. They were skinny, about seven feet tall, and had gray skin. Their eyes were very thin and yellow, their mouths had no lips, and their noses were flat. Rodríguez also noted that their hands, which were webbed to the first knuckle, had six long thin fingers and a thumb.

The "brain" being told Hodges that they were monitoring his

world because it had too much power, which was a reference to atomic bombs. On a large television screen, Hodges was shown different places on Earth highlighted with pinpoints of light, indicating places where humans could destroy themselves. Hodges was then shown a picture of a "dead" planet. Then he heard a buzzing sound and suddenly he was sitting in his car again.

Subsequently Hodges recalled having further encounters during which the humanoids told him they were from Zeta Reticulii and that the brainlike beings were "merely translators." But the many inaccurate prophesies they had conveyed led Hodges to conclude that the beings could not be trusted.

SOURCE: *Ann Druffel, "Encounter on Dapple Gray Lane," in* UFO Abductions, *ed., D. Scott Rogo (New York: Signet, 1980), pp. 160–182.*

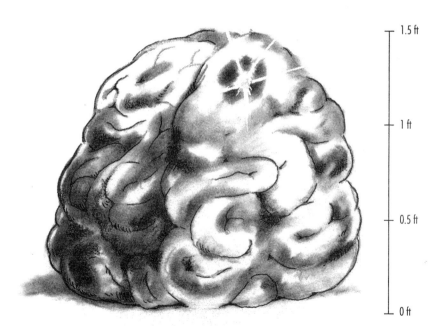

CLASS: *Exotic*
TYPE: *Physical*
VARIANT: *2, aka "Blob"*
DISTINGUISHING CHARACTERISTIC: *jelly "form"*

DESCRIPTIVE INCIDENT
DATE: *December 20, 1958*
LOCATION: *Domesten, Kristianstad, Sweden*
WITNESSES: *Stig Rydberg and Hans Gustafsson*

The witnesses spotted a mysterious glow in the woods as they were driving through a thick fog at three in the morning. When they stopped to investigate, they smelled a strange odor and spotted a disk-shaped craft resting on three legs on the ground. It was more than a dozen feet across and almost three feet high. But strangest of all were the four very odd beings hopping and jumping around the craft. These beings resembled jelly bags. They were about three feet tall and had no arms or legs.

For a while Rydberg and Gustafsson stood entranced by this sight when, quite suddenly, three of the bluish gray blobs fastened themselves on the witnesses and attempted to drag them back to the craft. One report mentioned that the beings had seized the men with rings or spirals, though this may have been a mistranslation of the tremendous suctionlike force the men experienced. In any case, the creatures smelled terrible, like a combination of ether and burned sausage.

The men tried to fight back, and at one point Rydberg sank his arm up to the elbow into one of the creatures. Rydberg managed to escape when the entities began focusing their attention on Gustafsson, who had been clinging to a post. When Rydberg returned to the car, he began sounding the car horn. The beings then dropped Gustafsson and shot like lightning back to their ship, which promptly departed with a high-pitched sound. The entire episode lasted about five minutes.

The men felt sick for three days, but a doctor who examined them found nothing wrong. Afterward the witnesses reported the incident to the Swedish Defense Staff, and the media had a field day with the bizarre story.

There are other cases of bloblike creatures seen in conjunction with UFOs in the literature, but most are by children. Some blobs glow green, or possess two black dots like eyes, or are filled with small circles similar to blood corpuscles.

SOURCE: *Douglas Hunt, "The Flying Jelly Bag Horror,"* Fate *(January 1960): pp. 68–71.*

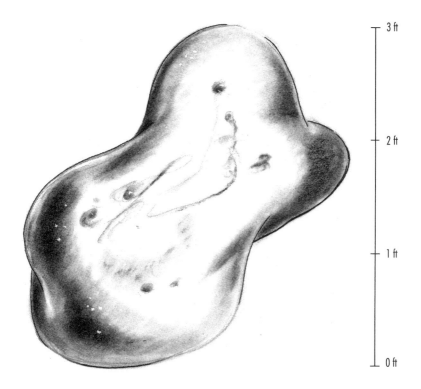

CLASS: *Exotic*
TYPE: *Apparitional*
VARIANT: *1, aka "ghost"*
DISTINGUISHING CHARACTERISTIC:
unformed appendages

DESCRIPTIVE INCIDENT
DATE: *November 12, 1976*
LOCATION: *Badajoz, Spain*
WITNESSES: *Three unnamed*
soldiers

Early in the morning two sentries in a guardhouse at the Talavera la Real Spanish air force base near the border with Portugal heard a whistling noise so intense that it hurt their ears. When they went out to investigate, they saw a bright light in the sky. A third sentry, who then joined them, also saw the light. The three, fearing sabotage, sounded the alarm and began to search the fuel stockpile area with a trained German shepherd.

Nothing occurred until they were struck by a blast of wind from what seemed to be a whirlwind. They then loaded their rifles and sent the dog into some bushes where they heard the sound of branches breaking. When the dog returned, it staggered, as if sick. After several more search attempts, the dog began to circle the sentries—the signal for danger.

Suddenly one of the soldiers turned around and came face-to-face with a "large" figure that appeared within an eerie green glow. The figure, which seemed to consist entirely of small points of light, was floating in midair. The heavyset creature stood about nine feet tall. Its head was small and covered by a helmet, but its legs and arms were indistinct, as if not fully formed.

The soldier thought of firing his rifle but suddenly lost his strength and eyesight, and he collapsed to the ground paralyzed. The other two soldiers, meanwhile, saw the figure and did manage to fire—about 50 rounds' worth—into the apparition. But suddenly there was a flash of light, and the ghostly entity simply disappeared. The whistling noise then sounded for another 15 seconds and stopped.

Strangely, an investigation that was mounted into the incident immediately after the shots were fired failed to find any trace of empty cartridge cases on the scene, or marks on the wall behind the entity, even though numerous people heard the shots. The affected soldier was later hospitalized for recurring headaches and loss of vision but eventually recovered.

SOURCE: *Juan José Benítez, "Encounter at Talavera,"* Flying Saucer Review *23, no. 5 (February 1978): pp. 3–5.*

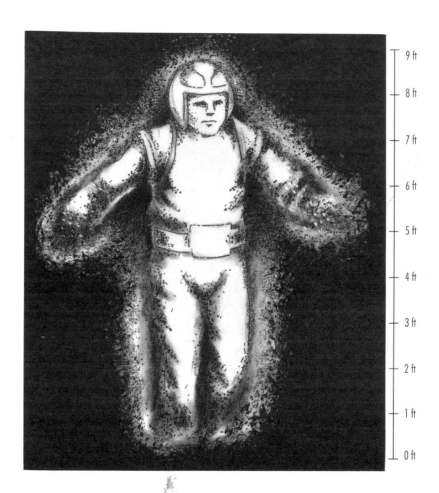

CLASS: *Exotic*
TYPE: *Apparitional*
VARIANT: *2*
DISTINGUISHING CHARACTERISTIC: *doubled appendages*

DESCRIPTIVE INCIDENT
DATE: *August 22, 1955*
LOCATION: *Riverside, California*
WITNESSES: *Kermit Douglas and seven other children*

At two in the afternoon, a group of children, ages four to 15, were playing in the yard of the Douglas family. While Kermit and another boy were wrestling, Kermit noticed a half-sun-like object in the air above them. After this object disappeared, a hovering silver disk appeared. Soon the other children noticed this object and others, semitransparent, like it, appearing and disappearing with a musical "ping."

What at first seemed like fun began to frighten the children. One of the objects, which bore a bright source of light on its antenna, landed in a field not far from them. The children saw a three-and-a-half-foot-tall being emerge from the craft. It had a big red mouth, big red eyes, and "four diamond-shaped things where his nose should be." When a seven-year-old boy started walking toward the object, two of the older boys tripped him up and prevented him from getting any closer.

Two boys also saw a transparent being about the size of a four-year-old child in front of the house next door. The creature also had those diamondlike spots on its face. The boys insisted that the creature was not standing on the ground but hovering above it. Another boy reported seeing an arm suspended in the air about 20 feet away and beckoning to him.

The strangest creature supposedly spoke to one of the boys. This being was solid-looking and wore satinlike clothing. Oddly enough, it had not only four legs but also an extraordinary doubling of the forearms; two forearms emerged at each elbow, one up, the other down. The creature told the boy to climb into a nearby tree, where they would pick him up in 15 minutes. When he and another boy climbed the tree, the other children forced them down using a garden hose. A few minutes later a bright craft flew around this particular tree, then disappeared.

The investigators felt that the children, who were frightened long afterward, told the truth—whatever that may be.

SOURCE: *Gordon Creighton, "The Extraordinary Happenings at Casa Blanca,"* Flying Saucer Review *13, no. 5 (September-October 1967): pp.16–18.*

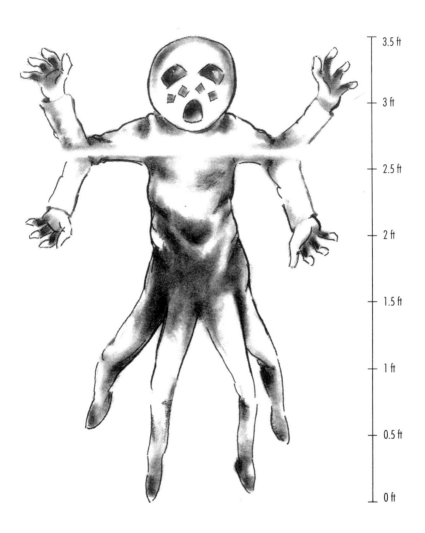

3.5 ft

3 ft

2.5 ft

2 ft

1.5 ft

1 ft

0.5 ft

0 ft

Too Human? Or Too Many Aliens?

You might doubt the extraterrestrial nature of many of the creatures in this field guide, especially if they look too familiar to you—too human, in other words. And you may be correct. Some experts believe that extraterrestrials would not look like us at all. Human physiology has evolved in response to a very narrow set of constraints, they argue. If Earth had started out with twice its present mass, humans would likely have developed with a stronger skeleton that may have precluded bipedalism. If the planet had started out with half its mass, our shape would also have been radically altered. Similarly, if the inclination of the equator had been 60 degrees instead of 23.5, or if our day was 100 hours long instead of 24, we humans would look considerably different. So how, the skeptics ask, could we expect creatures from a completely different planetary environment to resemble us?

But other equally qualified people believe that life elsewhere in the universe would indeed look very much like us. The late Cyril Ponnamperuma, who headed the University of Maryland's Laboratory of Chemical Evolution and was considered one of the premier scientists studying the development of life from nonlife, thought that the genetic code, which determines the appearance and makeup of all living things, did not originate by chance. He believed it evolved from a precise chemical interaction—one that would occur under the same conditions anywhere in the universe. "What this means," said Ponnamperuma, "is that extraterrestrial life is more likely to be chemically similar to life on this planet." The chemistry of the compounds making up the genetic code seems to demand that all life be similar. In other words, there's a natural tendency, like water running downhill, for the genetic code to produce life as we know it.

Regardless of the preponderance of humanoids, if this field guide is any indication of what's really out there, then we are certainly blessed—or cursed, as the case may be—with an overabundance of alien types. Taken at face value, one would have to conclude that the universe is teeming with space-faring civilizations from different planets visiting Earth. Of course, there really is no solid evidence that these UFO occupants are of extraterrestrial origin, though they certainly seem to want to give us that impression.

The descriptions of the aliens vary so greatly, in fact, that some regard this as a clue to their real nature as a product of the human imagination. Skeptics point out that there is almost as much physical variation in the appearance of the aliens as there are witnesses. While such a point of view may or may not be correct, it certainly highlights the basic assumption we hold about aliens: that they should have a consistent appearance. But one has only to look at the incredible variety of life on our own planet to see the flaw in this assumption.

The variety of life—even human life—on Earth is absolutely stunning. "We might pause to consider for a moment," notes Indiana folklorist Thomas Bullard in his unique study of abduction cases, "how a delegation of humans might bewilder aliens if we met them with representatives of our full diversity in age, sex, size, race, way of life, and individual differences."

Those Grays

But is the alien variety real? Temple University historian and abduction researcher David Jacobs thinks not. He believes the various types of aliens are confabulations, that the witness descriptions of the entities are for the most part mistaken. Jacobs thinks that the Grays are the only genuine aliens, though he does protect himself from the pitfalls of such a generalization by adding that "even if the witnesses are seeing different beings, it doesn't matter because they are all doing the same thing."

Jacobs sometimes distinguishes between two types of Grays. Those that are four and a half to five feet tall and those that are three to four feet tall. But despite some difference in appearance, notes Jacobs, since their general morphology is similar, they are probably of the same species. The beings have the standard complement of head, body, two hands, two arms, two legs, and two feet. They differ from humans in that they have only three or four fingers, no hair, no jaw, no ears other than a small hole on each side of the head perhaps, and no nose, though again there are reports of a ridge or holes where the nose would be. The mouth of the Grays is a mere slit that is not used for communication. Rarely does the mouth open, and when it does it fails to reveal teeth. Communication, if there is any, takes place telephatically, though Grays are generally vague and evasive, if not deliberately misleading—when responding to questions.

The eyes of the Grays are perhaps their most salient feature. Abnormally large, black, opaque, and fixed, their eyes have no whites, no eyebrows, no eyelashes, and no eyelids. Jacobs believes the Grays use their eyes "to conduct mental procedures" on the abductees. Biologists have pointed out that in nature when a creature has very large eyes it is because their environmental light levels are low. Consequently researchers have speculated that the short Grays must live in a world where there is much less sunlight than on our Earth. Such creatures would also have difficulties coping with our very bright sunlight, which might be the reason that about 90 percent of all alien contact cases take place at night.

The wrinkle-free faces of the Grays suggest to Jacobs that the beings perhaps do not age or, if they do, then not as we know it. Their skin is usually reported as gray, though not always, and either rubbery or plasticlike and without pores, hair, or wrinkles. The Grays' arms and legs seem to bend normally but are thin and frail. And there is some disagreement among abductees on whether or not their feet have toes.

Otherwise notable are features the Grays do not possess. Their bodies show no muscular development, and they display no visible bone structure such as ribs. Nor do they have hips, waists, breasts, nipples, buttocks, rectums, or apparent genitals. Though the differences between the sexes is not apparent among the Grays, abductees feel they can identify the sexes of the beings.

Their narrow chests, combined with the fact that abductees never report alien breath, bad or otherwise, even when they're just an inch or two from the alien face, suggest a lack of lungs. They are not air-breathing creatures, concludes Jacobs. Similarly, their morphology suggests that the Grays do not ingest food through their mouths for energy. There are no reports of an Adam's apple in their thin necks, there is no paunch where their stomach would be, and they appear to lack a rectum, all of which suggests to Jacobs that the Grays do not eat, at least as we know it.

Their thin tubular necks hardly seem capable of supporting their large bulbous craniums. The size of this cranium may be telling. In biology, cranial size is used as a rough measurement of brain development and intelligence. So perhaps the Grays are possessed of a high intellectual capacity. In any case, they are certainly sentient. They can make decisions, deal with crises, and perform specialized tasks.

"The composite picture that emerges from the many abductee accounts," writes Jacobs in *Secret Life*, "is of rational, logical, goal-oriented aliens who perform a variety of clearly outlined tasks with maximum efficiency in a detached, clinical manner. There is a hierarchical structure and a differentiation of labor. They are focused on human physiology, neurology, and reproduction. The aliens display very little sense of individuality. Their outward appearance is almost always the same, given the range of clothing types found. They volunteer no information about themselves. Although once in a while more complicated dialogue takes place, the consistency of their communication behavior suggests that they are carrying out a systematic policy of noninformation."

It's true, says Dan Wright, head of the Abduction Transcription Project, begun in the spring of 1992 by the Mutual UFO Network (MUFON) based in Seguin, Texas, that virtually every case has small Grays. But unlike Jacobs, he believes the Grays are by no means the only aliens around. "Always keep in mind," states Wright, "that we are dealing with multiple *groups* of entities who work together."

Beyond Looks

When there's more than a single entity involved in an encounter, the division of labor among the aliens (and alien types) becomes apparent. We get a glimpse of their social organization, their personalities, and their culture.

The most distinctive role observed in abduction accounts is that of the leader. This position is usually characterized by the entity's tall stature, some matter of distinctive dress—a cape perhaps—as well as certain behavioral qualities. The leader is frequently heard barking what seem to be orders at the other beings. He may even be distinguished by skin color. Wright notes that usually the darker the entity's skin tone, the higher his status.

The leader usually maintains communications with the human captive and has the closest relationship with him or her. Sometimes the leader also performs the more intricate medical procedures, as well as extremely close-up staring, which is known as the mindscan. The leader can be any of several alien types: insectoid, reptilian, even a darker colored Gray. If the leader is not the medical examiner, then this "doctor" has the second-most-obvious role among the aliens.

The only other distinct role is that of the crewman, who serves as the human escort, the guard, the ship's mechanic, or the specimen or soil collector. The pilots of the craft pay no attention to the subjects but attend to the controls exclusively. These tend to be Grays. For Wright, the Grays are the alien equivalent of worker bees. The Grays, he believes, are narrowly programmed. When confronted with unexpected human actions, they act confused. He thinks the Short Grays are low on the alien totem pole.

Despite this hierarchy of roles, however, folklorist Bullard notes that a democratic spirit seems to reign among the crews, as underlings are sometimes seen challenging their leaders with impunity. Disputes among the crews have been observed, and the beings have been seen to display a potential for anxiety and irritability.

Though the aliens exhibit a wide range of behaviors and emotions—from caring and humor to fear, surprise, confusion, sadness, curiosity, violence, and gratitude—for the most part, notes Bullard, the entities in UFO abductions maintain a clinical aloofness, a stone-faced lack of concern for their human captives. They are often inconsiderate, unsympathetic, and disrespectful of humans. Even angry witnesses fail to perturb them. Occasionally, however, something strikes their curiosity—the sight of a surgical scar or painted toenails perhaps—and their emotional temperature rises, if only slightly and momentarily. This, says Bullard, "bequeaths a vivid impression of strangers in a strange land, businesslike by training and temperament perhaps, but so new to the oddities of this world that humans were still full of surprises."

While the entities act without remorse in their examination of humans, they are otherwise often polite and sometimes even helpful. In a few instances an entity has acted to protect the abductee, usually from the rest of the crew. At times they even appear to be responsible for healing humans of one malady or another. An entity may on occasion reveal his or her name, though they are normally quite tight-lipped about themselves.

Yet there is a good deal of suspicion among abductees regarding just how genuine the goodwill of the aliens really is—especially if one considers their considerable record of false prophecies, outright lies, and deliberate deceptions. Most of the time, however, the entities simply avoid answering their captives' questions. One wonders, notes Bullard, if their behaviors are not all simply a matter of public relations or mind control.

They appear to be highly efficient and work oriented and will resort to any means at their disposal to manipulate the abductee into cooperation. But, notes Bullard, quite correctly, "a sense of shame for exploiting fellow intelligent creatures or tiredness after a long night's work in an unpleasant environment could just as easily explain the touchiness we sometimes observe."

Where Do They Come From? What Do They Want?

There are almost as many answers to the question "Where do they come from?" as there are witnesses. The answers come straight from the mouths or minds of the aliens themselves and from what the witnesses report seeing on their otherworldy journeys. Bullard, once again, has examined this question in considerable detail. More often than not, he discovered, the beings will not respond to this question, and even when they do, the answer is often meaningless or improbable. If the aliens are to be believed, Earth is being visited by more species than you can shake a stick at—aliens from Arcturus, emissaries from Orion, telepaths from the Pleiades, and reptoids from Sirius, among many, many others.

While at first glance this multiplicity of origins might make sense, considering the great variety in the beings' physical appearances, Bullard concludes quite rightly that what they say about where they are from is just garbage. The answers are offered obviously only to make the witness think they have an answer. In fact, most of the information provided by the beings, notes Bullard, "proves counterfeit and worthless." Their past predictions of war and mass landings have repeatedly failed to come true. Their "Earth is in danger" warnings are no different, or more helpful, than what we hear from environmentalists every day.

Leaving aside the "where," there is some data to tell us "what" their world is like. At times there is reference to intelligent beings living in domed cities. But most often there is a recurring reference to a barren planet and its desertlike features, with signs of devastation pointing to a natural or "alien-made" disaster. If this information can be trusted, then all is obviously not well with the aliens. On occasion they have actually said so—that they are searching for a new planet or that they are unable to reproduce and need humans for crossbreeding purposes.

Which brings us to, Why are they here? Well, in abduction cases, the central event is often the examination, with tissue and other samples being collected from human subjects. "Ankles, arms, feet, and the inside of the mouth were scraped; nails and locks of hair were clipped; and incisions or 'scoop'-type gouges were employed to remove flesh," reports Dan Wright.

Over the last decade, the apparent purpose of the abduction has dawned on researchers: the production of alien-human hybrids. The beings claim to want children. That appears to be their real concern. Nearly half of the subjects in the MUFON Abduction Transcription Project reported an alien interest in human reproductive systems and sexuality. "This included," notes project coordinator Wright, "harvesting sperm from males and ova from females, fetus abortion, and moments of sexual orgasm." Either the aliens cannot have children, or they are trying to create better beings through a breeding program with humans. Or they're just a bunch of sexual perverts.

Patterns

Long before metallic spacecraft and their occupants made the news, small beings from the otherworld were enshrined in folklore and mythology. Such creatures are in fact a nearly universal phenomenon. There are German dwarfs, Scandinavian elves, French *lutins,* Islamic *jinns,* Indian *devas,* Japanese *kappas,* Pygmy *mbefe,* Hawaiian *menehune,* Cherokee little people, and Inuit *ingnersiut.*

But the most familiar diminutive supernatural creatures are the fairies of Ireland, Scotland, and Wales, who manifest themselves as a host of species, subspecies, and races, including pixies, leprechauns, and brownies. And their parallels to modern UFO beings extend far beyond size comparisons. The little people often have large heads and eyes and pale skin, sometimes live in the sky, work at night, and have an inordinate interest in reproductive matters, seducing humans and giving birth to their offspring. "The humanoid," notes Bullard, "is a kind of malicious fairy in technological trappings."

But there are significant differences as well. Hairlessness is rare among supernatural creatures, as is the smooth, youthful look of many of the aliens. Fairies for the most part have an aged, wrinkled appearance—a look that is rare among aliens. So for Bullard the fact that humanoids resemble fairies may be more an act of chance than a tapping of the same spot in the psyche.

The look of the aliens has actually been affected somewhat by time and place. For instance, the Short Gray entity, although ubiquitous today, was largely absent from the UFO scene prior to the 1960s. The very earliest reports of entities involved primarily humanlike beings. And while the human types in the form of the blond "Nordics" were once responsible for about a quarter of the total cases, since the 1960s they have not been quite as common. Similarly, the hairy dwarfs that were reported so frequently in the 1950s are rather infrequent in contemporary accounts.

Author Jenny Randles has noted that prior to 1987, when Whitley Strieber's *Communion* and Budd Hopkins's *Intruders* were published in England, less than a quarter of the entities reported in Britain's abduction cases were of the small, bald-headed entities. But after the books appeared there, more than half of the cases involved the "American standardized alien," as she calls it. Because American abduction cases get more publicity than any other such cases, it seems as if the image of the Gray has been more or less imposed on the rest of the world as the standard alien type.

Not only has the appearance of the aliens changed over time, but the type of contacts that have taken place between humans and aliens is different as well. The earliest contacts were the simplest. Entities once avoided any encounter or relationship with humans who caught them unawares. Usually the aliens would be seen simply fixing their craft or collecting rock, soil, or water samples. The next stage of alien activity seemed to center on biological specimens, with dogs and cows drawing most of their attention. Then suddenly the witnesses themselves became the focus of the encounters, with medical examinations and sexual interests becoming the norm.

Similarly, the alien messages to humankind have changed over the years. They seem to have adapted to our own changing worries. In the early days they spouted antinuclear messages; today they voice more generalized environmental concerns. Prophetic or all too human? Actually, it's kind of a chicken-or-the-egg problem. The timing is such that it's difficult to tell whether human concerns have influenced the alien messages or whether the alien message presaged our own concerns.

Until the Gray was institutionalized as the prototypical alien by Hollywood and Madison Avenue, alien types also followed a distinct geographic distribution. From South America came reports of small swarthy dwarfs who were fairly aggressive, while from Europe and in particular, England, many reports were of tall blond blue-eyed beings with a much friendlier disposition. Meanwhile in North America the standard Short Gray with its shockingly indifferent disposition predominated. This once apparent geographical difference among alien types presents a major stumbling block to the reality of UFO extraterrestrials. The phenomenon seems to mold itself to conform to the culture and time in which it appears. This implies that the encounters are more likely visions than visitations by extraterrestrials.

Things Are Not What They Seem

There is now widespread suspicion among UFO researchers that things just aren't what they seem. David Jacobs, as I've noted, will admit that abductees report a variety of alien types, but he dismisses them. The only real aliens, he says, are the Gray alien. First of all, he argues, the vast majority of accounts in the United States are of those small Grays. Second, he says, aliens will plant false memories of themselves in the minds of abductees, and anything other than a Gray is very probably an incorrect memory. Third, abductees sometime confabulate, and improper questioning by the hypnotist may also lead to an erroneous description of the aliens.

Though I cannot fault Jacobs's description of the Gray type, I cannot agree with his conclusion that they are the only "real" alien beings. In fact, it's possible to use Jacobs's own arguments regarding alien memory control and eyewitness confabulation to argue that the Gray itself is but a cover for the aliens' real appearance. The image of the little Gray has become so ingrained in our culture with movies such as *Close Encounters of the Third Kind* that witnesses experiencing an encounter with an alien would quite naturally tend to see creatures in this mold, even if they actually are not.

So widespread is this image of the little Gray humanoid that researchers tend not to mention the "weirdos" that are reported to them anymore—the seven-foot-tall lizardlike creatures or the hairy troll-like creatures, for instance. This self-selection process tends to homogenize the types of beings investigators report and the public hears about. John Carpenter, a social worker in Missouri who has heard many encounter cases, admits quite readily that researchers relegate the other types of aliens to what he calls a "bulging gray basket." A few years ago Carpenter noted that he had 10 cases of seven-foot lizard-type beings, and none of the witnesses had ever heard of such a type before their own encounters. Can we hide them any longer, he asks?

Suspicions about what the aliens really look like have haunted UFO researchers for years. Some think that the human-looking entities, such as the blond "Nordics," might actually be screen memories imposed by the aliens. Behind the mentally imposed human mask lies the actual alien face, they say, though what the real underlying face looks like might be difficult to uncover. In one case, a witness told California psychologist Richard Boylan that she had encountered a "spaceman." When he invited her to look closely at the face of the "human" spaceman, she replied, "Oh my! It's not human after all. It's one of those Grays." But when he then suggested that she look closely at the face of the Gray, she realized that the Gray was actually a reptoid.

The real nature of these aliens is obviously quite elusive. One case in particular drives the point home. It took place on the night of May 30, 1974, in South Africa. When asked by the hypnotist what the aliens looked like, the witness replied, "They looked how I wanted them to look."

Evidence

When it comes to aliens, there is little certainty. Especially since there is no solid evidence that these UFO occupants are really extraterrestrial beings. We are the ones who claim that they are. We want them to be extraterrestrial. All of us: witnesses and skeptics alike.

"I would love it if there were aliens here," said Carl Sagan at a news conference in 1994, "even if they are a little short, sullen, grumpy, and sexually preoccupied....[But] people make mistakes, people misapprehend natural phenomena, people look for attention, money, or fame. People sometimes experience alternative states of consciousness—hallucinations are very common in all human beings, including normal people. And with that as the background, to really believe one of these cases you need really good physical evidence. And there is none."

That's true, of course. All we have are the stories we tell each other of those we have seen with our own eyes and call extraterrestrials. But for many of us, that's enough.

ACKNOWLEDGMENTS

Many people graciously contributed materials and ideas to this book. First and foremost among them is my friend Larry W. Bryant, who has nourished and sustained my interest in the UFO subject for three decades. Special thanks also to Loren Coleman for his help in tweaking my classification system, categorizing some of the more puzzling cases, and otherwise keeping me as zoologically correct as possible, considering the material; any faults that remain, however, are strictly my own.

Richard Heiden went above and beyond the call of duty by thoroughly searching his collection of that excellent journal *Flying Saucer Review** and providing me with the original published reports on which I have based many of the case descriptions in this book. Antonio Huneeus and Tom Benson were also kind enough to provide me with information I needed, even overnight in one case, to make a few last-minute corrections to my manuscript.

David George Gordon deserves a tip of the hat for unknowingly providing me with the inspiration for this field guide, and another goes to Thomas Bullard for his enormous, and enormously entertaining, analysis of UFO abduction cases. His work helped me get started on the selection of cases for this field guide, though I did not restrict myself by any means to abduction cases. And Victoria Lacas (now Alexander) deserves thanks, if for nothing else than for introducing me to Bullard's work many years ago.

I am also grateful to the many UFO researchers and writers whose work provided the foundation of this book, and I applaud the witnesses themselves for being courageous enough to come forward with their stories in the face of inevitable ridicule. I should also point out that many of the illustrations in this book are based either on sketches produced by the witnesses themselves or on drawings made by artists who worked in conjunction with the witnesses to reproduce what they had seen.

Finally I would like to thank Budd Hopkins, who in my many years of writing about UFOs has always been helpful, informative, and kind, even though we haven't always seen eye to eye on this wonderfully mysterious subject.

*Flying Saucer Review, *PO Box 162, High Wycombe, Bucks, HP13 5DZ, England.*

BIBLIOGRAPHY

(These references mainly support the Introduction and Afterword of this book, though they served as well to supplement the specific sources listed in the Field Guide descriptions.)

Banchs, Roberto E. and Oscar Adolfo Uriondo. "Idées Critiques sur la Classification de Jader U. Pereira," *Phénomènes Spatiaux* 37 (September 1973): pp. 30–31.

Barker, Gray. *They Knew Too Much About Flying Saucers.* New York: Tower, 1967.

Boylan, Richard J. *Close Extraterrestrial Encounters.* Tigard, Oregon: Wild Flower, 1994.

Bullard, Thomas E. *Comparative Analysis of UFO Abduction Reports and Catalog of Abductions.* Mt. Rainier, Maryland: Fund for UFO Research, 1987.

Carpenter, John. "Abduction Notes: Reptilians and Other Unmentionables," *MUFON UFO Journal* 300 (April 1993): pp. 10–11.

Clark, Jerome. *The Emergence of a Phenomenon: UFOs from the Beginning Through 1959. The UFO Encyclopedia. Vol. 2,* Detroit: Omnigraphics, 1992.

Culver, C. Leigh. "An Unforgettable Close Encounter," *UFO Encounters* 2, no. 3 (1994): pp. 3–7, 29–30.

Hall, Richard. *Uninvited Guests.* Santa Fe: Aurora Press, 1988.

Hough, Peter. "UFO Occupants." In *UFOs: 1947–1987.* Compiled and edited by Hilary Evans with John Spencer. London: Fortean Tomes, 1987.

Howe, Linda Moulton. *Glimpses of Other Realities. Vol. I, Facts and Eyewitnesses.* Huntingdon Valley, Pa.: LMH Productions, 1993.

Jacobs, David M. *Secret Life: Firsthand Accounts of UFO Abductions.* New York: Simon & Schuster, 1992.

Keel, John A. *The Complete Guide to Mysterious Beings.* New York: Doubleday, 1994.

Keel, John A. *UFOs: Operation Trojan Horse.* New York: Putnam, 1970.

Pereira, Jader U. "Les Extra-Terrestres," *Phénomènes Spatiaux,* special no. 2, 1974.

Picasso, Fabio. "Infrequent Types of South American Humanoids: Part 2," *Strange Magazine* 9 (spring-summer 1992): pp. 34–35, 55.

Pritchard, Andrea, David Pritchard, John E. Mack, Pam Casey, Claudia Yapp, eds. *Alien Discussions: Proceedings of the Abduction Study Conference.* Cambridge, Mass: North Cambridge, 1994.

Randles, Jenny. *Alien Contacts and Abductions.* New York: Sterling, 1994.

Ritchie, David. *UFO: The Definitive Guide to Unidentified Flying Objects and Related Phenomena.* New York: Facts on File, 1994.

Steiger, Brad. *Alien Meetings.* New York: Ace, 1978.

Story, Ronald D., ed. *The Encyclopedia of UFOs.* New York: Doubleday, 1980.

Vallee, Jacques. *Passport to Magonia: From Folklore to Flying Saucers.* Chicago: Regnery, 1969.

Wright, Dan. "The Entities: Initial Findings of the Abduction Transcription Project," parts 1 and 2, *MUFON UFO Journal* (February 1994): pp. 3–7; (March 1994): pp. 3–7.

Wright, Dan. "What We Know—and Don't—About the Entities," *Project Newsletter* (23 December, 1994).

Zurcher, Eric. *Les Apparitions D'Humanoïdes.* Nice: Alain Lefeuvre, 1979.

CASE INDEX

by date

135